Contents

Preface   ix

Roots and Wings   1

Speak to Me Only   5

The Magic in Mystery   23

Money Matters   28

Method in Our Madness   45

Making Music   66

Traveling   73

New Beginnings   83

Red Letter Days   91

Christmas   114

Food, Glorious Food   135

Index   155

Roots & Wings

Roots & Wings

A BOOK OF
FAMILY TRADITIONS

Helen Ream Bateman

Deseret Book Company
Salt Lake City, Utah

Library of Congress Cataloging in Publication Data

Bateman, Helen Ream, 1920-
   Roots and wings.

   Includes index.
   1. Family—Miscellanea. 2. Conduct of life—
Miscellanea. 3. Manners and customs—Miscellanea.
4. Interpersonal relations—Miscellanea. I. Title.
HQ734.B285   1983   306.8'5   83-1868
ISBN 0-87747-950-X

To my beloved family

Preface

I first conceived the idea for *Roots and Wings* while trying to find information to teach a unit on family traditions to my Family Life class of high school seniors. I found that little had been written about family traditions, yet their importance was emphasized by many authoritative books on the family. Sharing traditions in our classroom at Provo High School was so interesting to my students and so revealing of their influence on the family that I began to collect them, each year adding new ones and passing on to the class the most enjoyable and unusual ones from earlier classes.

I have drawn heavily on my own experiences in my family and in the families of friends and neighbors in order to write this book. I have talked with people on trains and planes from New York to California and from many walks of life. A few traditions have come from people I've met in other countries. Some I simply observed. All of them are presented here to help you create a more beautiful family tapestry, strong roots and wings for each of your children.

The title *Roots and Wings* was taken from a lovely birthday card created for me by my third daughter, Cindy, many years ago. She also contributed greatly by writing up some of the stories and lending her support and encouragement.

Kathy Bateman Peterson, daughter number two, drew all the illustrations. In fact this project reflects ideas, love, support, and help from Kim, Linda, Shauna, Rick, Kathy, Steve, Cindy, and Kyle. Most of all it could not have been finished without the encouragement and support of my best friend and husband, LaVar.

Special thanks to Carol Lynn Pearson for her keynote poem and some of her own traditions.

Many thanks also to all the students and friends who have shared their traditions so generously.

To you, my child,
An amazing blend
Of tree and bird—

I give two things:
For your staying—roots,
For your going—wings.

—Carol Lynn Pearson

Roots and Wings

A fascinating feat is the salmon's herculean effort to battle rapids and rocks in an upstream effort to reach home to spawn and then die. Much of what we know about that effort has been contributed by Dr. Arthur Hasler in his studies on the homing of salmon. His work was prompted by an incident in the Provo mountains when he was hiking there with his children. Coming around the bend on a mountain path, he smelled a meadow where he had played as a boy. The scent of the grasses, flowers, and water brought back the names of boyhood chums long forgotten and the games he'd played with them. *Art,* he thought, *you're a salmon and you're coming home!*

Most parents want to give their children the desire and the ability to venture into the world, to explore, to learn, and to achieve—to sprout wings and soar. We hope as they grow that they, like the salmon, will move into the great mainstreams of the world of challenge and adventure. We would like to know not only that we have given them wings so they are ready for the adventure, strong with developed talents, eager with awareness and curiosity, on course with faith and goals, and

1

sustained by a strong belief in self, but also that rooted deep within them are family values, traditions, and beliefs as instruments for homing.

As with the salmon, the homing instrument may be imprinted with sights, sounds, and tastes—love's memories flooding back with scent and sound and visual delight, to be lived over and over again, generation after generation.

Whole civilizations and cultures have survived or been destroyed depending on whether family life was strong and virile, or weak and dissipated. Family life seems to be weakening in many ways in this day and age. To ensure our survival as families, as a culture, and as a civilization, we must study and strengthen the forces that support family life. One of these forces is tradition. The most cohesive families are those with the most rituals and traditions.

The composite personality of the family is expressed through traditions, rituals, and practices, the little things that people invent and do, repeat and hold fast to, that add excitement, enchantment, charm, and fun, as well as stability, to the tapestry of living. They give family members a closeness and a sense of belonging, something to cling to, something to depend on. They are important consistencies in an inconsistent world.

The most successful families are those who do many things together; those in which the members are all good friends, who are comfortable, compatible, and companionable. Because many of their experiences are unique to them, they share a treasure of memories, traditions, and practices. They have their own language and private jokes. Three little pressures of the hand mean "I love you"; a wink and a glance mean that it's time to go home. All others remain outside the inner circle of this family love. One gains rare and precious insights when taken into that circle for even a moment.

Traditions are worth the bother, for they can enhance our self-image and give us a sense of belonging. They can assure us of our place in creation and renew the ties between ancestors and descendants, thus tying the past with the future. Remembering our origins in the past helps us establish firm roots in the present. Traditions can put delight into mundane tasks and help take care of the rough places in family life. They can affirm our love and caring. They can enhance our communication. Often these practices are so simple and seemingly insignificant that families do not even consciously recognize them as traditions. They would, however, miss them terribly if they were omitted.

When two people marry, a new family is born. This new family grows and matures in a healthy manner when the two take the best traditions from both families and blend them together into a family personality that is uniquely theirs, differing from either family of origin and often better than both. As a new or restructured family strives to introduce new practices and traditions, something they most want to establish as tradition may not take hold at all, yet something born accidentally or meant to be a one-time experience suddenly becomes a tradition. When someone in the family says, "We always do that," then a tradition has taken root.

Rituals seem to be the most exciting and fun when children are small. As the children grow up, outside interests pull them away to jobs, school, and marriage. The rituals then often taper off, to be born again in new families. In the closest, most cohesive families, however, this falling-away process is never a total one, because great effort is made by all members to continue the treasure of rituals. For example, one mother created a familiar "like home" birthday for her daughter, who was living in a dormitory at college, by arranging for a roommate to fill the room with balloons and serpentine and presenting the gifts at breakfast, just as the family did at home.

Traditions enhance the lives of parents as well as children and serve dozens of useful purposes. Our ability to build family traditions hinges upon making decisions and following through on them. Parents learn at some time or another that their children follow their example instead of their instructions. We learn that many of the things we do every day are the things that build our traditions, and they are the things that are handed on from generation to generation.

Strictly speaking, that's just what traditions are—rituals and practices that have been passed down from at least one generation to another. Many of the traditions in this book are so delightful and useful in rearing children that we wish we had heard them when our children were small and that we could have started them in our own family. That is why we want to share them with you. Some may only delight and amuse you; others, we hope, will be exactly what you need to help you give your child his homing instinct as well as his encouragement for flight—his roots and wings.

Speak to Me Only

Human relationships are delicate, precious, and fragile. Family relationships are doubly so, and communication between family members must be handled with great care. Of all human endeavors that fail, attempts to communicate are probably at the top of the list. Communication requires a sender and a receiver. The sender must send accurately, the receiver must receive accurately. Unless both succeed in their goals, correct communication is not achieved. It has been said that eighty percent of all the things senders try to communicate are incor-

rectly received. No wonder we have problems in human relationships.

Understanding is vital within families. To a large extent it
depends on the clear and accurate communication of true feelings and ideas among family members. To achieve this, we
need to sharpen our skills and call in all our resources. Words
are often inadequate, and when they are, we must find other
ways to convey our true meaning. Some of the other ways that
people have devised to communicate above and beyond the
ability of language follow.

THE STARRY-EYED BRIDE gasped with excitement and joy
at the boxes of orange blossoms and other exotic flowers the
bridegroom had brought from California for the wedding celebration. Her flair for the dramatic was totally expressed in the
joyous events of the day. After the honeymoon came busy days
of cleaning, sorting, and unpacking as bride and groom settled,
with an awkward newness, into the normal routine of life.

For the bridegroom, torn away from the fresh bliss of marriage by the demands of the working world, the change was
complicated by the inconvenience of strange surroundings.
The strain became evident when he asked one morning, in a
very accusing tone, "Where's my clean underwear, Lola?" It
was all dirty. The joys of marriage became slightly tarnished as
he unhappily and grudgingly pulled on some dirty underwear
and hustled himself off to work.

The new bride, feeling very alone with the tedious job of
bringing order out of chaos, and faced with the additional responsibility of dirty underwear, fumed through her wifely
chores. She was so angry that she would have gone home, but
she had no money. That night the honeymoon nest wore
icicles.

As the hours and then the days passed, she, the irresistible force, and he, the immovable object, wondered how they would ever find a happy meeting ground. She explored the alternatives. Go back to Utah to face family and friends? Not without money. Besides, she had made some pretty solemn promises before God and man. Live on in this cold atmosphere? Impossible! Then the answer began to tug at her heart. An apple pie! He could never resist one, and it was the crown jewel of her culinary skills.

That night even the enchanting smell of apple pie wafting through every room in the house could not move the stubborn bridegroom, and the lovely dinner progressed in stony silence. But then she brought the pie in—warm and golden. The immovable object softened, crying, "Lola, you do love me?" And then she was in his arms.

Throughout fifty years of marriage and eight children, Lola's pie has been the white flag of peace, a secret, yet unmistakable message of love bound by tradition and time. To one family an apple pie might mean Sunday dinner, to another it is only a dessert, but to this couple it's a white flag of truce saying plainly, "I'm tired of this fight. Let's kiss and make up."

WE INVENTED a sensitivity meter. It's an imaginary device with a scale of one to ten. If someone says, "I'm on a scale of nine today," the other family members know to tread lightly and use kid-glove treatment. If two people disclose that their scales read two or three, they can tease, romp, jab, and play, knowing that the other will understand and have fun too. We've come to depend on our sensitivity meter to cue us in to each other's feelings. Our lives are richer and smoother because we've learned to share our feelings.

EARLY IN OUR MARRIAGE we learned that it is very easy, after a difficult day when nothing goes right, to speak too sharply and snap back in return. Before long we would find ourselves entangled in a fruitless word battle. We made a pact. If my husband was feeling cross and irritable, he turned his tie around when he came in the door. His backwards tie was my clue to treat him gently, walk softly, and do everything I could to soothe and lift his spirits. When I had my apron on backwards, he read the message clearly, took the children off my hands, and perhaps suggested a special date. If, when I greeted him at the door, we both wore the backwards sign, it either brought a laugh and a sharing of the day's problems, or we tactfully avoided any irritating contact until time had calmed the storm.

FAMILIES MAY LIVE under the same roof and remain strangers or become antagonists. Little family rituals and practices can open the doors to deep communication and lead to greater love, harmony, and understanding. Often the problem is not lack of love, but that love is unexpressed or misinterpreted. The song "Do You Love Me?" from *Fiddler on the Roof* rang a note of identification and understanding in our ears and reminded us that it is not enough just to love; one must show his love in some way.

"BUT I'M ALMOST SIXTEEN, Mom," Kathy pleaded, her eyes betraying hopeful dreams. "He's a student-body officer, you know his parents, and he won't be eighteen for months." Despite the mother's upraised eyebrows, the tiny seed was planted.

Steve graduated, and that summer the quiescent seed was brought to life. The shy beginning years fell away, and Kathy reached the dating age. Many times he dropped by unannounced and whisked her off for an ice-cream cone. The family grew to know and love his casual charm, the lively evening piano concerts, the canyon picnics, and his gallant admiration. Although he knew she dated others, he patiently came by nearly every day. Each time when she returned from a date she found a soft-drink bottle on the back step with a daisy propped awkwardly in its long neck. "It was all I could find," he'd say later, shrugging with a playful smile.

Steve was Kathy's first date, her first kiss, her first love. Then, when the leaves of autumn began to change color and wither, he went to Japan. The two-year stay was the test of drought for the spindly seedling. As days passed, she busied herself with the distracting bustle of high school and the excitement of new dates and new friends. Letters came and went, but, oceans apart, they corresponded in cheerful generalities.

Then one day a package from Japan arrived, addressed to Kathy's mother. She smiled at the instructions and the odd contents within. On her daughter's birthday, her mother crept quietly into Kathy's bedroom and carried out the instructions. She'd barely left the room when Kathy woke, rubbed her eyes, and stretched. Suddenly her sleepy eyes widened. There beside the bed sat a small green bottle with Japanese characters on one side and the familiar soft-drink label on the other. A tall, lanky daisy still swayed slowly, as if a silent hand had reached across the vast ocean and placed it there moments before. Tears and an excited squeal brought the family running. The small glass bottle whispered a thousand united thoughts, and the daisy, a wealth of future dreams.

In a few days the flower wilted. The bottle was eventually buried with other keepsakes. But two years later Kathy and Steve were married. Even now whenever the need for a special message of love crops up, the soft-drink bottle and the daisy appear.

WE SECRETLY TUCK little love messages in someone's pocket. Usually they are written on impulse when one of us feels special appreciation or wants to encourage. It's a rule that when we find one that has been given to us, within twenty-four hours we must write one for someone else. Sometimes it is quite a while before a note is found, but whenever it is, it brings a needed lift and a special warm feeling of being loved.

ONE DAY as I was doing my housework, I felt an overwhelming appreciation for all that my husband meant to me. Instead of just letting the feeling pass, I sat down and captured my mood in a little letter and sent it to his office. This started such good things happening that I've kept it up through the years, not regularly but spontaneously, usually two or three times a month. It brightens his day and takes the drudgery out of reading his business mail. It's made our marriage sing!

WHEN PRESSURES MOUNT and sleepless nights turn cheerful faces into exhausted scowls, we play a little game that always brightens the scene. We leave love messages on our mirrors, written with the edge of a bar of soap. They aren't hard to wipe off, so no one worries about the soapy mirror. Scrawled notices are often treasured there for days before being wiped reluctantly away. But even though they are erased from the mirrors, they never seem to be erased from the heart and memory.

WHEN I SEE my older brother for the first time in quite a while, I always run and jump into his arms, and he swings me around. Even now, although I am seventeen and he has three children of his own, we still do it. I hope we do it forever.

OUR THREE-YEAR-OLD DAUGHTER started a family tradition. One day I asked, "How much do you love me?" Her face lit up, and in an all-out effort to express the love in her childish heart, she exclaimed, "I love you big as the whole sky—many!" That is what we tell each other still: "I love you big as the whole sky—many."

TOAST WITH FROZEN RASPBERRY JAM has always been a royal treat at our house. Inevitably, when the toast and jam are ready to be passed to a hungry little brother, older hands grasp it first, but only for a moment. The dripping toast, minus one large bite, always reaches the youngster with an unspoken message of tolerance and love.

When Martin opens his carefully packed lunch, it isn't just the Twinkie or dill pickle that makes him smile. A love bite in the middle of his sandwich says in secret code, "I love you, we share, and I'm a tease."

A PERSISTENT YOUNG MAN, who was trying to persuade me to marry him, had a hundred pictures of himself printed up. He and my roommate hid them everywhere in my room. If I pulled out a handkerchief to wipe a tear, there was his face saying "I love you." If I opened a book or took a dress from the hanger, there was my true love's smiling face, asking my hand in marriage. I married him! Those pictures were just the beginning of the lovely ways he has told me of his love.

DAD WAS A SCHOOLTEACHER. He and Mother made their lives rich in everything but money. In the fifty-seven years of my parents' marriage, my father never failed to give my mother a Wednesday Surprise. Their marriage began on a Wednesday, and he never stopped celebrating with a gift for her. In all those years, he never duplicated the gifts except for candy and flowers, which he varied as to type and kind. The gifts ranged all the way from clever little things he found in the drugstore to two tickets to Hawaii.

MANY FAMILIES use little message rituals that others can't decode. Occasionally when you notice one, such as a wife's wink to her husband to tell him it's time to go, you feel almost as though you have intruded on a private conversation.

Real traditions never die with age. Our family never seems to tire of our secret whistle. It is a discreet little "tweet" that only trained ears can hear and practiced tongues can chirp.

A well-articulated tweet catches the ears of another family member anywhere within hearing distance. In fact, the tweet has come to mean so many things that it is practically a complete form of communication when combined with smiles, winks, eyebrow wiggles, and eye-to-eye contact. When a family member walks into a crowded room, a single tweet is enough to stretch just the right heads above the crowd for a moment of enlightenment before they dive back into a sea of unfamiliar faces.

At parades, funerals, church, or school, tweeters can keep in touch with scarcely a disapproving glance from outsiders. After all, how often do you notice the birds chirping? It is a secret message of reassurance between two sisters at a school dance. It drifts over the heads of the congregation to an anxious younger brother waiting to speak in church. It brings instant relief to one who is shorter than the countertops and lost in a crowded department store. This subtle and very selective form of communication has given an extra touch of binding identity to our family.

IN THE OLD DAYS of the telephone party line, our number was one long and one short ring. This became a secret identifying signal that still packs a lot of meaning. When our car drives up, the toooot-toot announces just who is there. We use it to communicate family support, coded hellos, and many other little messages.

MY FATHER HAD A WAY of communicating with a teaspoonful of water. He found it useful on all kinds of occasions. After he had filled a dessert spoon with water, he would hold the handle away from him in his left hand, with the index finger of his right hand on the tip of the bowl of the spoon. When his right finger slid off and the left hand gave the handle a flip, the contents of the spoon flew across the room into the face of the surprised offender. I always wondered how long he had to practice to aim with such amazing accuracy.

If we lingered too long after a reminder for bedtime, a well-placed splatter sent us scattering to our rooms, sheepishly wiping the water from our faces as we went. We knew it was half in fun, but we also knew he meant it.

The trick was especially handy for cooling off an argument that was getting a bit too heated. Dad was usually so sly that we rarely saw him dip his spoon into a glass and poise it for action.

But if we did, the formidable spoon and the look on his face were sufficient to trigger an immediate change of behavior. The element of surprise was part of its effectiveness.

MY PERCEPTIVE HUSBAND knows how much I hate to iron. The dampened clothes lie rolled up in a big basket, just daring me to find the bottom. Then one day, when I was halfway through the batch, I found a candy bar and a love note from my husband tucked among his shirts. It was a joy to do the rest of the ironing; I was doing it for him. We use this little technique to surprise and encourage each other and to help make routine jobs more fun.

SURFACE TALK and small talk take relationships nowhere. To really know each other, we must share on a deeper level. Some families seem to do it naturally; some plan deliberately to make it happen.

When the adults in our family get together, we share special moments of the past week or month or however long we've been apart. Mother or Dad usually starts by asking, "What is the most special thing that has happened to you in the past month?" Then we all take turns telling. This procedure eliminates the small talk when our time together is short. It gets us deep inside the heart and builds fresh admiration, empathy, and love.

FOR AS LONG as I can remember, the girls in our family have congregated in the bathroom for the nightly ceremony of brushing teeth, putting up hair, and other feminine rituals. We had only one bathroom, and it was lots more fun to share than to wait. Perched on the edge of the tub or sitting crosslegged on the floor, we discussed our dreams, solved problems, shared bits of gossip, and whispered exciting secrets. It was there that we talked about our dates and even our plans to marry. We cried about our hurts, our joys, and our tender moments with lots of toilet paper handy to blow noses and wipe each other's tears away. These sessions were never planned—they just happened. The men of the family smiled with tolerance, not quite understanding. Now my own girls are married and come home only for visits. And often young husbands give up waiting and go to bed alone, with the bathroom sessions still in progress.

WE BARGAIN FOR BACK RUBS at our house. You scratch me and I'll scratch you. It is really just an excuse. Rubbing backs on the floor in front of the fireplace seems to knock down all the barriers and open us up to sharing our thoughts and concerns. The loving touch of a good back rub communicates caring and opens up the heart to healing and sharing.

MY MOTHER STARTED DANCING to music with us when we were very small. She held us tight in her arms, and the dipping and whirling and laughing made us feel very close. Sometimes we would crash down on the couch in a heap of laughter at the end. As we got bigger, we danced with our feet on the floor. Even now that I'm a senior in high school, when we are working at dishes or something, I'll feel a tug on my arm, and Mom and I will whirl away and dance.

WHEN SOMEONE IN OUR FAMILY has some exciting news to tell, he writes it in a letter and then cuts the letter into a jigsaw puzzle. The suspense mounts as the receiver finds a matching edge for each piece. For really big announcements, the pieces are sometimes mailed home in separate envelopes.

A RECENT STUDY indicated that the average father spends less than seven minutes each week alone with his individual children. If that is true, is it any wonder that family communications break down? In contrast, many fathers hold a personal interview at least once a month with each family member. Without exception, those who do so report that it is a rewarding experience for both parent and child, and is also a key factor in building family unity.

Some families find that a good time for interviews is the first Sunday of every month. Often, despite efforts to create an atmosphere of acceptance, love, and understanding, it takes a few sessions before children will share openly. But eventually paths of real communication open up and are built into patterns that go with the children throughout life.

Physical contact can add to the enjoyment and closeness of the experience. When a child is small, he may perch on his father's lap or just sit close, with the father's arm around his shoulder. This contact says "I care a lot about you," no matter what grave matters are being discussed. Effective interviews go a long way in training family members to face problems rather than retreat, and to be open and honest rather than belligerent and devious.

Some families also use this special time for goal setting. After Father conducts the interviews, Mother might encourage each child to choose both short- and long-range goals. Progress is evaluated at the next monthly interview, and adjustments or new goals are made.

An evaluation is held at the end of each month by both parents, when achievement of goals is noted and rewarded. Evaluation also helps encourage children to follow through with their commitments. Families may find themselves working together to help achieve one another's goals. A spirit of cooperation and love permeates the home and makes living there a rich experience of work and growth. Parents and children develop a binding interaction with each other that is honest and accepting.

FOR HUSBAND AND WIFE prime time alone is often hard to find, and sometimes during the busy years of child-rearing, it seems almost impossible. As our children were growing up, we tried to grasp every chance to be together we could find. At our house it was a treat to share errands. "I have to go to the store," my husband would call. "Jump in the car and go with me." I dropped whatever I was doing to go with him, and even the inconvenience of arranging for the children was made worthwhile by the moments we shared—just the two of us.

WHILE WE WERE STRUGGLING in graduate school at Yale, my husband and I found little time together. I felt trapped with three small children, no friends in a strange town, and the burden of an over-squeezed budget. One stressful day he surprised me with an unexpected entrance and this startling announcement: "This is *your* afternoon; I'll tend the kids."

Where could I go? What could I do? I didn't know anyone, and I had no money. Smiling, he gave me a map of the Yale library and marked a certain table with a star. Puzzled, I drove to the library. As I hesitantly approached the table, my eyes fell upon a stack of six carefully selected books with a candy bar on top. That afternoon I felt excited and grateful as I escaped into the books. But far more lasting was the warm feeling of love that had made the day all mine.

After that, whenever he could squeeze out the time for "my afternoon," he would set it up for me. Even now that the children are grown and beyond needing my constant care, a gift of an afternoon planned by my husband fills my cup to overflowing.

MOTHER HELD NURSERY SCHOOL in our house and was dearly loved by all the children. With so many children vying for her attention, she wanted to do something for her own children that would communicate to them her great love above and beyond what she felt for her nursery-school children. That's when she invented our Nights Up.

Each of her six children would choose a night when he could stay up for an hour beyond the bedtime of the others and have a special hour alone with Mother, and sometimes Father too. The extended bedtime always came too quickly and usually caught us sliding a final batch of wild-looking cookies into the oven, snuggling together on the couch with a story just reaching its most exciting point, or intently gazing at a few remaining chess pieces in a carefully drawn-out game. Nights Up took a lot of dedication—and sometimes sacrifice—on my mother's part. Occasionally someone's Night Up had to be scrapped for a high-priority emergency, but generally we kept to our schedule. We all gained a sense of importance and learned to come to Mom with all our most pressing problems.

Nights Up eventually came to mean any special time together. I remember Dad would say, "Let's have Nights Up. Come with me while I referee the basketball game." In that precious time together, I learned all the technicalities of the game, and I gained insights into an official's joys and disappointments. But most of all, I learned to know and love my father on a one-to-one basis. We still have Nights Up whenever we can, though our childhood days are far behind.

WE WRITE "ROUND-ROBIN" LETTERS that circulate among our family members, from youngest to oldest, about once a month. When the envelope with the letters arrives, the recipient reads them all, takes out his own old one, and puts in a new one. We each try to include news of interest to everyone as well as snapshots, news clippings, and sometimes even a favorite recipe. We have a rule that if any family keeps the letter more than three days, they must include enough postage for the whole circle for one letter. Sending the letter back out again within twenty-four hours is a point of honor with us. The letters are so interesting that we really look forward to receiving them. This is a great way to keep in touch with families, and by saving the letters and filing them as they've completed their round, we each have a little history of our family events.

OUR GRANDPARENTS loved to read stories to us before they moved far away. We all missed the stories so much that they began an experiment that grew into a tradition. Each month

they buy a lovely storybook, and then Grandmother reads it
into a tape recorder complete with "turn the page now" so that
even the little children can follow the book as they listen to the
tapes. When the story is finished, if there is room on the tape,
she and Grandpa tell stories about their own lives. They seem
to be right here with us. We are making a library of children's
books and tapes. We plan to save them for the next generation,
so that those children will know their great-grandmother's
voice and stories.

MY HUSBAND AND I decided before our wedding that
Thursday would be a special day for changing and growing together. After we had turned out all the lights and retired, and
we were in each other's arms, we would take turns naming one
thing the other was doing that was irritating, and ask him or her
to change it. The irritation had to be something that could be
changed. We ruled that the request must be said lovingly and
accepted in the same way.

We have continued this practice throughout the ten years
of our marriage. It has been a good tool for us for solving serious
differences as well as small, irritating ones, such as draping
bathroom towels sloppily on the tub. The other six days of the
week we work on being very positive and supportive and building each other up.

OUR SEVEN-YEAR-OLD MARRIAGE seemed to be slipping
into dull routine. We had stopped talking about important
ideas, and our lives seemed to revolve around minutiae. The
steps we took to revitalize our companionship were awkward at
first, but gradually they became traditions we cherish. First, my
husband made it his responsibility to bring to the dinner table

each night an interesting idea to stimulate discussion. We love it, and even the children join in by bringing things they want to talk about.

Second, each January we choose six or eight books that interest both of us to be read during the year. Since we don't have time to read together, we each read on our own time schedule, underlining things we like or want to discuss, writing little notes to each other in the margins, or leaving notes in the book. Sometimes these books furnish some of the discussion at dinner. These discussions often lead to teaching moments for the children, as we comment on moral issues. We save the weightier ideas that are beyond the understanding or interest of the children for special sharing at bedtime or for walks. Reading the same things and sharing our opinions and ideas have helped us grow together.

The Magic in Mystery

The crystal chandelier hung glittering above our heads, sending a myriad of little rainbows across the tall ceiling of the department store. Breathlessly, my two teenage daughters whispered, "Oh, buy it, Mom, it's perfect for our new dining room!" Even though I could see that the blues and orchids of those iridescent crystals would lend just the right touch of class to our newly decorated dining room, I could also see just as clearly that our tight budget had little room for glittery dreams. We turned reluctantly away.

Two days later, the doorbell rang, and I was confronted with a large box on the doorstep. A note on the box said, "For the Bateman family." The box was not closed tightly, and amid the crushed tissue I caught the unmistakable gleam of those same iridescent crystals. The whole family gathered at my call, and with gasps of delight, the chandelier was uncovered. Dad's protesting voice was heard but not heeded: "Don't take it out! It's a mistake; we can't afford it!"

When we inquired at the department store, we were told, "Yes, it was bought for you and sent as a gift. We are not at liberty to say who it is from."

For months we tried to solve that mystery. Whom should we thank? Only a handful of people even knew we had longed for that chandelier. We found ourselves suspecting everyone, and as we did, we built warm bridges of love and respect with many friends. I still don't know who gave us that chandelier, and I'll never ask, because that might spoil this special family mystery that has brought so much enchantment into our home.

A little mystery adds intrigue and excitement to otherwise dull moments of life. Small mysteries are easy to devise. Dad may bring home something in a brown paper bag that no one can see until after dinner. Mom may make a special surprise dessert. Simple things, yet they bring magic to the moment.

In one family the parents taught their children that Christmas and giving mean more when they invest a little time to make their own gifts. When they began their project, a considerable amount of pride and competition in the making of the gifts became evident, and the father noticed that the givers were basking too much in the glory of their gifts. "At Christmastime," he announced, "we should pay more attention to the spirit of Matthew 6:3: 'When thou doest alms, let not thy left hand know what thy right hand doeth.' We should give without taking credit for the gift." The family then agreed not only to make their own gifts, but also to give them anonymously. This added another element of mystery that seemed to multiply the fun. The unanswered question—"Was it you who did that nice thing for me?"—permeated all family relationships.

As the family grew and new members were added to the clan, the tradition continued to flourish. Unusual wrapping paper camouflaged oddly shaped boxes. Typed cards, disguised handwriting, and mysterious delivery techniques all contributed to the secrecy.

A few years ago, the young son of the family, by then married and a graduate student at a university, was delighted when a friend agreed to let him use his dentistry equipment to cast and polish a lovely gold ring for his wife. He carried the ring home in his pocket and gave it to his father to wrap and tag. On Christmas morning the father rather ceremoniously placed the camouflaged package under the tree. Supposing the gift was from her father-in-law, the young wife kissed and thanked him for it several times that day.

The rules of the game say you don't have to own up to giving the gift or deny it. This time, however, the father couldn't resist sharing with his son the credit for that special gift, and thus he gave the true giver away.

YOU'VE HEARD OF PIXIES. They're little people who are sensitive to others' wants and needs and who give service in small secret acts of kindness. Our house needed one (every house does), so I made a little pixie, dressed him in a cloak made of tiny blue forget-me-nots, and put him on our mantel. Magic things began to happen as each family member watched for a chance to do a secret good deed for someone.

One morning as I went to my room to do my morning

chores, I found my bed already neatly made and resting on my pillow a forget-me-not, the pixie's "autograph."

Susan had a very busy study schedule exam week and desperately wanted to finish her new skirt for the Friday dance. There just wasn't time, but when she started to dress for the dance, the new skirt lay on her bed, topped with a tiny forget-me-not.

John was so busy with the school play that he wondered how he could ever get his lawns cut. Dutifully he set the alarm for five, but when he turned it off, he saw the note signed with the forget-me-not. "You are a great lawn cutter, but this time I beat you to it. Catch another forty winks. You need to be fresh for the play tonight."

The pixie's "autographs" are kept in a little crystal bowl on our hall table. No one assigns our pixie; he is spontaneous. But if he hasn't made an appearance for a while, when he does appear, a sudden rash of pixie goodness pops up everywhere. It's catching!

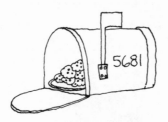

IN OUR NEIGHBORHOOD at Christmastime one year, we planned an activity that has since become a family tradition.

All afternoon my daughters made cookies and delicious treats while the boys planned escape routes and "drop" procedures. As soon as it was dark enough for a safe getaway, the whole family gathered to make their deliveries and leave the treats in neighbors' mailboxes. Early the next morning a disguised voice called each "victim" and reported the sneaky deed. As the tradition has continued, with each cookie drop the entire neighborhood becomes a buzz of friendly gossip about the "Phantom Family."

We decided that part of the adventure is seeing that it continues to be undetected. Whenever anyone starts to suspect or make accusations, we plan a Phantom Family project to be carried out by secret helpers while we go out of town. After being thrown off the track, no one can guess who the Phantom Family really is.

Once while we were out of town for a few weeks, there was a rash of vandalized mailboxes in the neighborhood. Unaware of the problem, we resumed our Phantom Family projects. The first one was to a neighbor whose house is within sight of our own. We watched her look of surprise the next morning when she went to her mailbox, but our smiles suddenly faded as police sirens filled the air and a bomb-squad van screeched to a halt in front of her home. Three or four policemen leaped from the van and approached the mailbox. With extreme caution, the officers slowly opened the hinged mailbox door. To their surprise, the neighbor's chagrin, and our delight, there sat a plate of cookies.

OCCASIONALLY MY HUSBAND springs a surprise on me. He takes an afternoon off work and rushes home announcing that he is stir crazy. He'll take off my apron or unplug my iron, and whatever I'm doing will stop. Then he'll swoop me out of the house and away to an adventure he has planned. It's fun to be gently commandeered into an afternoon of freedom away from life's fray. When the children were small, he'd even arrange for the baby-sitter. Whether it's a few hours in the autumn leaves or a new show that has just come to town or a cross-country ski tour, such adventures color our life with sunshine.

Money Matters

Marriage is like the corporate merger of two people who have very different views toward money and different methods of handling it. The needs and demands of children are a further complication. Those families that are most successful in financial management seem to be able to resolve their differences and develop these common qualities: good communication, refusal to go into debt, willingness to plan ahead, and reasonable expectations. Many families have developed interesting and productive practices and traditions that indicate their attitudes about money and the way it is used. Learning ways to increase family income and to use what we have to the greatest advantage of every family member not only improves the present family, but also prepares the children to handle their own finances in the future.

In teaching high school seniors about money management, I've learned a great deal myself. Consistent teaching about money management seems to be woefully lacking in many families. Very few of my students have money of their own to manage until they have jobs. Occasionally, though, a class member will share a family practice or tradition that is designed to help the children learn some important skill of money management. The following one excited me so much that I wanted to turn back the clock and try it with my own children.

GOOD MONEY MANAGEMENT PRINCIPLES were put to work early in our family. Each of the seven children was given a small allowance to manage from the time he or she was six. Our parents gave us jobs where we could earn and taught us to spend wisely. Dad has a sharp eye for good real estate buys. Upon graduation from high school, each of us in turn has helped him choose a duplex that could be purchased with a reasonable down payment. Our parents then helped us as young graduates to borrow money for the down payment and was a cosigner with us. Rent from each duplex helped pay off the mortgage and even enabled us to pay off the loan for the down payment. The duplex then belonged to us, with the upkeep and care our responsibility.

This wise investment cost our parents little except the loan of their financial credibility. But what a boost it was to us! It was our start in life. It was training in how to succeed. As we left home for marriage, jobs, or school, we could live in one side of the duplex and rent the other, rent both sides, or sell the building for the equity. The venture proved to be a great lesson in management, responsibility, and good enterprise in every case. We all want to continue the tradition in our own families.

GIFTS AT OUR HOUSE are often shares of stock. Our children then become junior partners in our country's economic system. They become interested in stock price changes, company earnings, how each business is run, and the business's economic growth. By consulting experts and choosing stocks carefully, we have learned that such gifts can last a long time and teach many lessons. Some stocks that we bought as penny stocks later became quite valuable. The children quickly learn that it's exciting to save by investing. They've also learned the importance of going to experts for advice on money matters. It's also important to learn that one should invest only what he can afford to lose.

WITH THE ADVICE OF EXPERTS, we organized our family into a corporation to accomplish some exciting goals. We also formed a limited partnership. Some of the spinoffs will be tax shelters and funds for special needs, such as college. One of the factors that prompted us to do this was the problems relating to property that arose at the death of our parents. Death is traditionally a time of crisis financially as well as emotionally in families. With our organization, few of those problems will exist. The children are already partners in all that we have, and everything is provided for in case of our death. We have a corporation business meeting at least once a year. We make this a special occasion by going out for dinner, where we can relax and enjoy one another's company. This has been rewarding in family togetherness and loyalty, and the cost of the dinner is tax deductible.

We feel this is one of the most important family traditions

we have started. Now we are a team even legally. The most important thing to remember is to hire a lawyer who is an expert in this type of financial planning so that he can help you accomplish your goals and adjust your plan as your family grows.

WHENEVER ONE OF US broke a neighbor's window or caused other damage, we weren't afraid to go home for help. Our parents recognized two important facts: first, that even if the damage was caused by carelessness, the destruction was usually not intentional, and second, that paying back a large amount is overwhelming to a child. They used these times to teach us that we do need to make restitution when we have caused pain or loss to another person. Just as important, because of our family's way of handling these problems, we learned about family solidarity. Three rings of our bell summoned the family. When we had all gathered, the problem was explained simply, without scolding or casting blame, and we discussed what we could do to help the one in trouble. A good plan was always devised that wasn't too hard on anyone, though it often rquired some sacrifice from all. Our family stands unitedly, each sacrificing to help another through difficult times.

SOMETIMES IT IS DIFFICULT to keep families close after the children leave home, but some families know how to do it.

Our family fund grows every year. Dad started it with a base of $1,000, and each adult family member adds $120 a year. In case of death, sickness, or weddings, we send gifts paid for from the family fund. Emergency funds are also available to help family members who might need them. When the borrower is able, he repays his loan so that funds will be available for some-one else.

ATTITUDES TOWARD MONEY are sometimes the most im-portant things we learn. Often there is disparity between what children want and what parents are able to give. Children may easily develop an attitude of envy toward their friends.

Our father and mother gave us a weapon against envy. We grew up in a neighborhood where the other children all had more money to spend than we did. Whenever envy's head reared itself, we talked about it. Somehow envy dissipated more quickly when we discussed it. Usually at dinner Mom or Dad would skillfully discuss with us our values and the things we prized and worked for. We learned to choose our priorities. Then we would talk about how we must work to obtain the things that meant the most to us. We were taught that not hav-ing things we wanted and couldn't have might sometimes make us feel inferior, while choosing not to have something in order to work for something else could make us feel superior. When we felt superior to possessions, envy was gone.

WHENEVER MONEY began to assume too much importance at our house, we reminded each other that money is just a medium of exchange. We grew up knowing that money is im-portant for achieving some of our goals. We also knew that neither happiness nor pleasure was dependent on money. To prove this, we had a "no-money" fun night once a week. We discovered that often the things that are the most pleasurable don't cost a cent. One night we all sat on the curb in front of the house and sang songs. Soon many of the neighbors joined us. Someone brought a little mandolin, and we sang and laughed and talked far into the night. It was an experience we'll never forget.

SOME FAMILIES RAISE MONEY for family needs by bringing to family reunions clothes and other items to be auctioned off or traded. The proceeds are often used to finance the reunion or for genealogical research. One family writes up family histories and stories complete with pictures, sells them at handsome prices, and donates the money to the family cause.

STAYING OUT OF DEBT is a tradition in our family. Our motto is "Saving precedes spending." On our kitchen wall hangs a poster that says "If your outgo exceeds your income, then your upkeep will be your downfall."

We believe that attitude is more important than happenings, and we try to make the best of everything. We refuse to be unhappy or miserable. As Abraham Lincoln said, "You can be as happy as you make up your mind to be." Our happiness is never dependent upon how much money we have.

ONE OF THE ASSIGNMENTS in our high school class was for
the students to sit down with their parents and plan a budget for
a month. Seventeen-year-old Steve, who had loudly criticized
his father for being an impossible tightwad, expressed a total
change of attitude the next day in class. "I don't know how they
manage to live from month to month," he said. Just knowing
what it took to make house payments and pay for food, utilities,
insurance, and so forth, changed his attitude from always trying
to get what he wanted to understanding and helpfulness.

Some families make it a practice each month to share the
financial plans with all the family, from the time the children
are big enough to show any interest or need to share in the family resources. Children can be taught early to honor family pri-
vacy by not talking about private family business.

SATURDAY NIGHT was the time our family got together to
go over family finances for the week, pass out allowances, and
discuss financial goals and needs. Mom always prepared a simple supper of potato soup and a surprise dessert. We all remember with a special feeling of pride that we were important
members of our family team.

Another family that held a family finance report night be-
lieved in profit sharing. Each child received his share of the
family business profits, which were put in the bank for his future.

A BANK ACCOUNT is opened for each child in our family on
the child's sixth birthday. A deposit of five dollars is made, and
the child is then encouraged to keep the account growing on

his own initiative. At age six he is also given a small allowance and the opportunity to earn money by performing a chore in the house or yard. He is taught to pay a tithing of one tenth of all that he receives. One-tenth is also set aside for his bank account. He may spend the rest as he chooses. This practice is an important part of the training of our children. At first the amounts are very small, but as the children grow in their ability to work and produce, so do they grow in wisdom as to how to use the money they have.

I BUY MANY CLOTHING ITEMS for myself and my children at Good Will, Deseret Industries, and other secondhand stores. The children love these "spending sprees." We make it a special day out together. For a very small amount of money they can have many nice things. Some of my favorite clothes are from such outlets.

A doctor's family that we know also shop at the secondhand stores. They would rather buy property and take trips to Europe than spend money on expensive clothes.

OUR PARENTS TAUGHT US how to make a spending plan for our money. At the beginning of each month we had a family meeting at which we were given our allowance and made our spending plan for the month. Our very simple budget looked like the chart on the following page.

If our planned expenses exceeded our income, we discussed ways we could supplement our income by doing odd jobs. We also discussed ways we could improve our spending practices. We considered doing without or making items we needed or buying items at thrift or secondhand stores. We often extended our clothing budget with make-overs. We kept a supply of old

My Spending Plan								
Expenses	First Week Date _____		Second Week Date _____		Third Week Date _____		Fourth Week Date _____	
Fixed	Planned	Spent	Planned	Spent	Planned	Spent	Planned	Spent
Savings Contributions School lunches Transportation Other _____ _____ _____ _____								
Flexible								
Hobbies Movies Snacks Books Gifts Grooming aids Clothing Sports Other _____ _____								
Totals								

things that still had good materials for that purpose. We unpicked, washed, pressed, and schemed to get it cut out. It was fun to get something for nothing—nothing but work, that is.

WE TAUGHT OUR CHILDREN that if they were willing to work for free for a while to get training and prove themselves, the practice would eventually pay off. Jobs are always available for those who will work for nothing. Sometimes prospective employers were hard to convince, but no one turns down free labor if you persist. The children worked eight hours a day dependably as if they were getting paid. They became eager volunteers and gladly learned their jobs. Eventually someone recognized their skills and virtues and offered them a job. They had jobs when no one else did. The apprenticeships paid off.

WHEN OUR CHILDREN WERE SMALL, their constant begging to go to the store to buy treats concerned me. They were spending all their allowance and hard-earned money on junk. To help them learn how to use their money more wisely, I decorated a box and labeled it the Family Store. Twice a week I filled the box with their favorite treats, some homemade and some that I bought. The children took turns being the store manager, and all the proceeds from their purchases at the "family store" were put in a bank to save for a family trip. They learned how much they were spending and how their savings could increase. We eliminated the tension from the constant pleadings to go to the store, and the Family Store became a growing experience for all of us. It was such a favorite tradition that even as the kids grew older we kept it up.

A CAREFULLY PLANNED BUDGET doesn't always balance when there are teenagers in the family. With our three oldest in high school, my purse was always drained. I struggled to keep enough cash available to meet their needs. Clothes, school functions, books, dates, piano lessons, cheerleading uniforms, band trips, band instruments, and gasoline seemed to eat up our savings. Something had to be done. Out of necessity a tradition was developed.

We held family council meeting one night and suggested that the older children each make a list of their physical needs for the year. How many pairs of shoes did they need each year? What kinds? How many jeans, T-shirts, pants, and dresses? How much would the items cost? We tried to stimulate their thinking with suggestions and comments based on our past experience.

When the lists seemed complete, we totaled each list for the year and divided that figure by twelve. This final figure was to be their monthly allowance. Faces brightened at the sight of such a figure, especially when it was agreed that school books, school fees, and music lessons were to come from a separate family fund. We made special arrangements for money earned during the summer. For instance, if a son had a summer job and saved all of his earned wages, his allowance was to continue throughout the summer. But if he spent his extra money unwisely or carelessly, then no allowance would be granted in the summer months.

Before our family council meeting was over, each child received a budget book with instructions on how to carefully record every cent spent during the month. We did not criticize what the children spent their money on as long as each purchase was accurately and honestly reported. Before anyone received the next month's allowance, he had to report to his father and account for his last month's expenses.

Elated when they saw how much they would have each month, the children eagerly began to make their shopping lists. But experience soon taught them that money goes fast when you don't plan and budget. Gradually three carefree teenagers began to hunt for good bargains and responsible purchases.

With each passing month, the atmosphere of our family seemed to improve. As parents, we were no longer on the defensive when it came to money. The children were the ones who had to analyze their needs and make the crucial decisions. The monthly meetings with their father to report their spending and to receive their allowance were special times that helped develop communication and harmony.

Many things were gained from this tradition. Each child came to appreciate why we parents are so concerned with wise purchases and balanced budgets. My husband and I gained a better understanding of a teenager's financial needs as we read and approved their organized books. Each member of the family learned how to use that budget book to tally total expenses and balance the income and the outgo. When faced with a self-written description of their monthly expenditures, the children realized how much they were spending and gained a healthy appreciation for budgeting and planning.

WE REQUIRED EVERY CHILD to do certain jobs around the house without pay as their contribution to family welfare and to show love for one another. My husband would post in the kitchen a long list of jobs that needed to be done around the house or yard. Each job had a price tag on it. The children would sign their names beside the jobs they wanted to do and the date they planned to complete each job. If they didn't get the job done by the deadline date, another person could claim the job and its reward. The jobs ranged all the way from such chores as digging the dandelions out of the lawn to big ones like painting the outside of the house. We learned to be good workers and to keep our money in the family.

JOBS WERE SCARCE around our town, so my father and mother helped us evaluate our salable talents. We decided that anything we could do for love, we could do for money. We drew up lists of things we could do and distributed them around the neighborhood. A local merchant even let us post one in his window. We always had plenty of jobs.

PART OF OUR YARD became a small truck garden for our family. Every year we shared with our children the problems and profits as we worked the land together. Some preferred to dig, weed, and harvest; others enjoyed selling and delivering the produce; and one enjoyed keeping the records. The children learned about themselves as well as the skills of gardening and marketing. At Thanksgiving time we divided the profits and gave thanks.

SAVING FOR A PURPOSE is better than just saving. Our family held planning sessions to set goals, which were then posted in our rooms. We set both short-term and long-term goals. If money was needed to reach a goal, plans were made to obtain the money to accomplish it. Often our parents assisted by providing jobs or helping us to find them. Sometimes they even offered to pay part of the amount we needed or match what we earned. We always felt their support, and we came to believe that we could accomplish any goal we set. As we progressed toward our goals, we reported on our progress and made new goals.

DO-IT-YOURSELF PROJECTS provide opportunities for every member of our family to learn to make simple repairs. We all learn to repair electric cords, faucets, flat tires, and fan belts, and to darn socks with holes in them. Seldom is a task too difficult for our confident fingers. Through such projects, we have become better consumers, and we also save a great deal of money.

WE DISCOVERED that we could save about twenty percent of our food budget if we shopped only once a month. We plan ahead and shop the first week of the month, except for perishables. We pick those up once a week.

EVERY SPRING we hold a family garage sale. We have a chance to get rid of things we have outgrown or no longer need, unclutter our lives, and also line our pockets with a little cash. We have made as much as two hundred dollars at a single sale.

ONE FATHER CONTACTED business acquaintances to help his son Mike line up lawns to cut and yards to groom. Mike built a fine reputation, and soon his father's friends in the real estate business were asking him to care for property listed for

sale or rent. Mike's grandfather, aware of the ease with which
cash can disappear, matched every dollar that was deposited
safely in the bank. By the time Mike graduated from high
school, he had five thousand dollars in the bank. Matching the
children's money that they banked for long-range goals became
a family tradition.

TRADITIONS ARE GREAT for teaching gospel principles,
such as the parable of the talents. On the first of November we
give our children ten dollars each. They have a month to see
what they can do with their money. Anyone who doubles it
gets an extra ten to spend for Christmas. If they can triple their
fortune, their reward is twenty dollars. When the children are
small, we help them find projects that can help multiply their
investment. Sometimes two of them will combine their resources on a joint project. This custom has helped all of our
children become very enterprising.

WE WERE HAVING DIFFICULTY living on the money coming in, so we decided on a family business that would utilize our
talents to bring in extra cash. We started a candy and catering
business. With mother's flair for fancy foods, cake decorating,
and candy, we soon had more business than we could handle.
Serving and helping provided jobs for young cousins and neighbors. We started the business on a shoestring, taking small
catering jobs and then buying equipment as we could afford it
to expand to bigger jobs.

SOME PEOPLE call it "Sweat Equity"; we call it home. But if we did want to sell our home, there would be a lot of equity above and beyond the cash we've put into it.

Coming from a family with do-it-yourself tradition has its advantages. We borrowed from an uncle the money to build the house, promising that as soon as the house was finished, we would refinance it and pay him back. We knew nothing about building, so we hired a carpenter who had some experience to work with and teach us as we went. He agreed, providing we were willing to work twelve hours a day with him. We subcontracted big jobs, like the cement-work footings and basement, electrical wiring, and plumbing. We quarried the stone from the family ranch in Idaho, sharing the beauty of nature and the power of man as we cut the giant stones. It has been said that if a marriage can survive building a house together, it can survive anything. For us, it was an exhausting, demanding adventure filled with rewards that we are still enjoying after twenty-five years.

IN OUR FAMILY it was the custom that when anyone announced that he wanted to get married, Dad would say, "Fine! We'll help you. The first requirement is that you manage the household for one month." That included buying groceries, cooking, doing the laundry, and cleaning. Family members could be asked to help, but the responsibility rested on the shoulders of the bride- or bridegroom-to-be. A future bridegroom had to pay all the bills and take care of the yard and car as well as help with the house. Dad, of course, still signed the checks. The first one to take this test was quite young, but our parents voiced no objections. They didn't have to. Two weeks after the experiment began, she came to Dad and said, "I've changed my mind. I'm not ready for marriage." This enlightening experience tends to weed out the romantics who aren't ready to take on the responsibilities of marriage from the mature ones who are ready.

Method in Our Madness

The family has the awesome task of providing for the optimum growth of each member emotionally, physically, socially, intellectually, and spiritually. Its challenge is to teach "how to" in countless areas: how to become dependable, self-reliant, self-assured; how to be creative, cooperative, productive, and so on. The list is endless.

This chapter is about traditions that have been devised to accomplish some of these goals or tasks more constructively.

WE WANTED OUR DAUGHTERS to learn how to sew well, so we decided that any piece of material in our house belonged to whoever sewed it first. We have a drawer filled with stacks of assorted fabrics, some that we find on sale and others that we just can't resist. Anyone can have a piece of material from the drawer if she wants to sew, but a project must be finished before another one can be started. Clothes may be purchased at the store, but money for them comes from allowances or wages. On the other hand, to encourage sewing, material is always free and available for our daughters. If supplies get low and selection is limited, more is purchased. Needless to say, the girls in our family are excellent seamstresses.

BECAUSE PARENTS are their children's first and most important self-interpreters, we have the power to develop in them a strong self-image. If they have high self-esteem, they are prepared to add the other qualities and skills they need. Some of the ways we can assure the development of a strong self-image are: show our children respect and appreciation, give them success experiences daily, spend time with them alone, and reward their good behavior and teach them how to overcome the bad.

Creative thinking and persistence are necessary to accomplish these goals and turn them into tradition.

Living within two hours of Chicago was a great experience for our family. Once a year each of mother's six children was treated to a special spree in the city with her. The sprees were not in celebration of a birthday or special holiday; they were our special time with mother. I discovered that she didn't do this just for us—she loved it too, and that made it even more wonderful. We always took a bus or train. That in itself was fun, especially having breakfast on the train, but even more important, it freed mother from driving. She gave us her undivided attention from the moment we left until we arrived back home again, delirious with exhaustion and loaded with stories to tell for months. We spent the time going to Chicago reading books and brochures about things to do there, and we got to do the choosing. We took in museums, shopped, slept, and shared little secrets. We felt there were just the two of us in the whole wonderful world.

Mother had another little custom to make us each aware of our own importance: a monthly date to do something of our choice in our own town. This helped teach us how to budget our time, for she was a very busy woman, prominent in church and community affairs. How proud we were of her, and how we loved these super times with her.

IN OUR FAMILY we declare "Be-kind-to-Mary Week" (or John or Jane or whoever needs it). Once in a while everyone has a bad day. When spirits are low and self-image is deflated, there's no better medicine than "Be-kind-to-me Week." Dad declares it, and everyone in the family tries to do something nice for the honored person every day that week. With miraculous speed, the broken ego is inflated and a healthy balance of self-confidence is restored. It is amazing what a little special attention will accomplish.

WE BUILD THE SELF-IMAGE of each other by accentuating
the positive. When we were first married, we were determined
to keep the great admiration we had for each other and not let it
slip away as we had noticed in so many marriages. We each
made a list of all the good qualities we saw in each other. Then
we put the lists in two frames and hung them in our bedroom.
When we are upset at each other, the lists help us remember
the good things. To keep the lists growing, each year on New
Year's Day we review them and add new items we have discovered during the year. Then we each draw up a resolution of one
new virtue we would like to build in ourselves, and we help
each other by discussing our progress on our goals the first day of
each month. Sometimes when we think we've conquered one
goal, we add a new one.

WE DISPLAY ARTWORK of our children for a few days; then
it is put away in a folder. Once a year we go through each child's
folder and help him pick out a few of the best pieces to save; the
rest are thrown away. We are careful to date everything so that
we have a good record of each child's progress. The items are
saved in the child's own file, a large box he helped to decorate.

AWKWARD SITUATIONS are often breeding grounds for
new traditions. For instance, one winter I took a group of high
school students on a midnight snowshoeing trip to a friend's
cabin. The moon was beautiful and full, the night a delightful
picture of newfallen snow and graceful silhouettes. For nearly

five miles we puffed and plodded along. The first mile or two still held the excitement and mystery of such a splendid adventure. But as time wore on, tired legs could scarcely drag nearly frozen toes from drift to drift up the mountainside. And our backpacks were no help either. Every few minutes someone's snowshoe straps would come loose or break, sending that person flying into the snowbank head first, a feeling akin to being tripped with your feet tied together and an elephant on your back. No one really complained much, though, because we all knew that a warm cabin was waiting at the top.

When we finally reached the cabin and worked the old door open, we gasped as we looked around. Windows were broken, the kitchen table had three legs and a stump, three rusty springs showed through the upholstery on the couch, and the cabin itself seemed unbearably small. After a moment of awkward silence, someone in the back of the group begged us to go inside. Maybe it wouldn't seem so bad when the place was warmed up. With little optimism we went to work.

Months before, someone had left the chimney flue open, and frozen snow was jammed in the fireplace all the way to the roof. One person doggedly picked away at this solid block with a pocketknife while I went to the kitchen to start the wood-burning stove. Disaster again! The stovepipe had separated and was also packed with snow. It was frighteningly cold, and the cabin was quickly filling with the choking smoke. Everyone was complaining and feeling sorry for themselves.

"Hey," I shouted, "there's a new rule. For every complaint you make, you've got to say something good as well." More grumbles. "Well, what have we got to lose? We can at least die with a positive attitude."

"But I'm freezing," one person complained. I smiled and waited patiently. "Uh," he choked, "but at least the smoke is warming the place up."

"Three of the four windows are broken," a girl grumbled.

But then she brightened. "At least they draw out the smoke. Should we break the other one?" That brought a real laugh.

As I poked in the fire, billows of smoke seeped from every crack in the old stove. I hoped it would melt some of the ice above. After unloading each armload of wood, I would rush to open the door and draw a few fresh breaths of cold mountain air. Two girls alternately fanned the fire and dashed for the door to breathe, while the boys struggled with the broken stovepipe upstairs.

Gradually the smoke began to clear. As the snow in the stovepipe melted, the cabin warmed up and so did our spirits. Before long we had a big pot of hot soup on the stove, and the youths were sitting cheerfully on their rolled-out sleeping bags, sipping hot chocolate.

The next morning, we started down the mountain we had climbed in the dark. Walking became difficult, so we sat down on our seats, braking with our snowshoes propped under our arms, and slid down the mountainside all the way to the parking lot.

Without exception, our memories of this trip are filled with excitement, peril, and adventure. No one seems to remember the grumbles or the complaints. Now we have a family policy that whenever an awkward and potentially disastrous situation confronts us, we have to say something positive after each grumbling complaint.

I HAD A FAVORITE TRICK for handling my three children, age four and under, when they were too tired, cross, and hungry to be good table companions. I filled the big sinks in our kitchen with warm, soothing bubble bath and popped them in with a couple of little toys. Sometimes we sang songs to keep them busy while I filled their plates. Frowns turned to laughter, and baths and dinner were finished in much gaiety. Bibs were unnecessary—the spills just splashed away. Later, when they were a bit older and too big for the sink, we had special bathtub suppers. I'd bring the food in on a tray and tell them stories as I sat on the floor, steadied the tray, and supervised the eating.

This was an effective way to get the children fed and to bed on nights we went out or when we wanted to have a candlelight supper alone. Now the children are doing it with their own little ones.

WHENEVER WE QUARRELED at our house, Mother would hand us each a spray bottle and a pile of newspapers and set us to washing windows, one on the outside and one on the inside. We couldn't quit until the windows were sparkling. We would start out crying and making faces, but we always ended up laughing and working together. Our windows were always clean, and many a quarrel found a quick solution when someone reminded, "Shh, or we'll have to wash a window."

OUR FAMILY BELIEVES that when a conflict occurs between children, *they* should solve the problem. It is their problem, not the parents', and the best solution can come from them. Often, the worst decision they arrive at is superior to the best decision an interfering adult might produce, and much more workable.

A room in our home is designated the "Solve-it-yourself Room." Whenever a conflict arises, the persons involved go to that room and stay until they have arrived at a solution acceptable to both. The only rule is that no physical "solving" is allowed; all sparring must be verbal.

At first we worried about our three-year-old being able to

hold her own with the older children. However, she soon
learned how to defend her rights. For teaching children to stick
to their beliefs and defend them, to make rational decisions,
and to untangle crucial conflicts, the "Solve-it" room is excellent.

IN THE CURVE of our parents' grand piano sat a beautiful
chair, but when they died and the furniture was divided, no
family member wanted it. Memories flooded back to frustrating
times spent there learning one of life's most valuable lessons:
how to say "I'm sorry" and really mean it. According to the rule
in our house, when anyone was angry or hateful, they had to sit
it out in the "mad chair." The length of stay depended on how
soon the angry one could say "I'm sorry" from the heart. Now
saying "I'm sorry" is easy for me. I took the "mad chair."

IF A BOY gets in trouble in our family, his uncles "kidnap"
him and escort him up to their ranch. There, with much ten-
derness and love, they discuss the matter and work out the
problem until it is solved. No one returns home until all present
can communicate freely and feel good about the solution.

ON COLD WINTERY NIGHTS, if we put our pajamas on fast,
we were allowed to play Blow by the Blanket. Mother would
throw a blanket over the furnace vent, and we'd all get under it
as the heat billowed the blanket up around us. We loved to stay
there till we were toasty warm and rosy cheeked; then father
would bundle us off to bed.

GRANDMOTHER'S OLD ROCKING CHAIR became the seat of a family tradition. I loved to rock my baby to the creak of the rockers while singing an age-old lullaby. One day, on impulse, I propped her tiny body carefully in the chair and took a picture. The results were so delightful that we decided to do it every year on her birthday. In subsequent years, we carefully made the setting and distance the same, and the total sequence created a growth record that speaks more eloquently than words. In the last two shots she sat there as a bride and then with a baby of her own. The tradition has stretched into the second generation.

WE LOVED OUR WEDDING PICTURE so much, as we stood together proud and tall, that we decided part of every anniversary celebration would be to take a picture in which we posed in the fashions of the day. We try not to be too classical but to wear the most modish thing we have to show the changing styles. Those pictures mounted and framed are the conversation piece of our home.

PICTURES OF FAMILY MEMBERS at every age hang in our hall, so they can watch themselves grow up before their eyes. When the whole family gets together, we always take a tallest-to-the-shortest picture.

WHENEVER A RELATIVE comes to visit with our family, we drag out the home movies from the past thirty years. With a sheet taped to one wall, we watch all our films from beginning to end. Every time we come to the part where Uncle Parley is dancing around the campfire, playing an old fiddle at one of the family reunions, Dad switches the projector so the film runs backwards. We all laugh and shriek as if it were the first time we'd seen it done that way.

ONE OF OUR CHOICEST POSSESSIONS is a tape made by a neighbor of a story told by our three-year-old. We can almost hear the wheels turn in his head as he struggles to make up the story as he goes along. No picture could ever capture the creative nature of our child as that tape did. We have several other family tapes that we never tire of hearing. How we wish we had done as one family who wrote: "Tapes of children are as great as pictures. We tape a record of them and their doings at least twice a year, always on each birthday and again on New Year's Day."

WE CAPTURE THE MAGIC of special times with parents and grandparents on our tape recorder. The tapes are a link to our family ancestry and record stories that make our progenitors live for us and the children. Taping is most successful when we conduct interviews to spark their memories. To know ourselves, we need to know our ancestors, both living and dead. We have found that to know them is to love and appreciate them.

THE MEMORY WALL is a beloved element of our family traditions. Every important event in the family, from school plays to family trips, is represented with snapshots, programs, marked-up road maps, or souvenirs. These mementoes aren't tucked away in boxes or drawers to be forgotten; they are artistically displayed on a wall at the bottom of our stairs, a collage of instant memory ticklers that awaken a flood of reminiscence. One look at the hand-carved love spoon from Wales or our honeymoon airline tickets is enough to light a smile and take my spirit far afield while I push the vacuum cleaner.

WHATEVER HOUSE we live in, mother, an artist, paints a great spreading tree in the front hallway, and on its branches are hung small pictures of all the family members, in little gold frames. The goal is to help the family members know their roots and to feel a strong sense of belonging.

OUR LOVELY FINNISH MOTHER punctuated our days with her colorful way of saying things. One day my brother put up on the wall in the kitchen a large piece of paper and titled it Mama's Dictionary. There he wrote her idioms and sayings. "It's rubber boot weather" we would hear her call, as we pulled on our school clothes on a drizzly morning. All these special little sayings, along with family jokes, took their place in Mama's Dictionary. It hung there till it yellowed with the years and captured our children's special language too.

WE LEARNED TO SHOW AFFECTION in certain ways because of the way our family did. Mother always woke us with a kiss. We always kissed good-bye. Affection was expressed in gifts brought home from trips and gifts given when we visited friends and relatives. We often made a game of hiding gifts and hunting for them. But best of all, we always jumped in bed with our mother and father on holidays and weekends, and they took us into the warm circle of their love. When we got married, we bought king-sized beds, big enough to hold the whole family.

WHEN THE FAMILY all gathers together, we play table games, such as Monopoly, Risk, and Rook—sometimes until the early morning hours. The refrigerator is stocked with soft drinks, sandwiches, and other munchies to be devoured as the great competitive evening progresses.

OUR GRANDMOTHER didn't think it was right to pass sweet treats and junk food around when she came to visit. She really loved us and wanted her visits to be exciting, remembered, binding ones, so she made a Grandma Bag. Buried in its depths were dozens of intriguing things: a slate to write on, paper, tape and glue, books, stories, and sometimes little trinkets from her treasures of the past. But the real gift she brought us was herself and her time. She'd sit right down, spread open her bag, and help us do all the exciting things she had planned.

APPRECIATION OF THE WORLD AROUND US was a tradition in our family. Our parents wanted to make us more aware of our surroundings. We watched together as graceful wings carried a bird in his wide swoops and glides above the sea. A sudden dive, then he was aloft again, triumphant with his treasure in his beak. Mother helped us see the wonder of the world and the joy of being *us* with her delighted cry, "Oh, they knew we were coming, and they did it all for us." She was a showman to the last inch, and the glories of the world around us became uniquely ours.

ON OUR "PEOPLE NIGHT," members of my family dress up according to the customs of a country we are studying. Mother goes all out to teach us about people from Holland, Japan, Mexico, and many others, including our own American Indians. We eat a carefully planned menu of strange imported foods that try our tastebuds and expand our interests. Sometimes we invite friends to share the fun.

PROMPTED BY THE FACT that their children were growing up without much knowledge or appreciation of their grandparents and uncles and aunts, our parents designed a plan to get to know relatives who lived far away. They set aside days of the year to honor absent family members. On those days they would tell stories from the honored relative's life, show pictures, serve the relative's favorite foods, and even call him on the telephone. Sometimes we made tapes or wrote letters to send to the honored one. The children's hearts warmed toward their relatives, and they began to get excited about reunions.

OUR FAMILY HAS BUILT slide-sound presentations of our family history, to which we add a new chapter each year. The presentations help the children and new in-laws to know and understand the family. These presentations are the highlight of our family reunions. Even the little children love to watch them.

OUR REUNIONS are held for a whole week every year, on property owned by one of the relatives. He has created a private campground by the small river that runs through his land. The river has good fishing, and each year all that are caught are measured, and a handsome rod and reel is awarded to the one who catches the biggest fish. The competition keeps the younger ones occupied for long, lazy hours, and allows time for uninterrupted visiting for the adults. The children usually beat the adults in the traditional softball game, and then it's turn-about when the adults win in the horseshoe competition. A prize is given to the family that keeps the neatest campground. Meals are shared on a huge table, with menus planned ahead of time and food contributed by all. We wouldn't trade our week at the family get-together for any other vacation. We also all get together for a Christmas party in December.

THE MOST PAINFUL PUNISHMENT I can recall from child-hood was the time my father said, "All right, if you won't do your tasks, we'll just relieve you of them, and you won't be able to help with anything for a whole week." What a joy, I thought, to just be able to play for a whole week and not do any work.

But suddenly I found myself outside the family circle. They all seemed to have such fun working together. They asked each other to do things, but never did they ask me to bring this or do that. I didn't last the long week through. "Please, Dad, could I just help you pick up this trash and clean the yard?" I guess he knew that the punishment had made its point. He smiled and let me help, and not another word was said. But how I loved the work we shared that day. I had not known how important work was in our family, and Dad taught me in a way I never forgot.

Much satisfaction in adult life comes not through recre-ation, but through dedication to significant causes or work done well. We need to provide children with challenges and opportunities for development. We need to help them learn that everyone needs a balance of work and play; and that most of life's greatest satisfactions come through accomplishing something difficult against great odds or pressures. When they can define a goal and reach it, or plan a task and complete it, children are on the road to self-control and self-mastery.

MY BROTHERS AND SISTERS and their families love to help one another. We believe that anything is possible if we are united. One of the ways we do this is with a "steak and rake" party. If a family has a yard to clean up or a big job to do, we all bring tools and help. Then the host family furnishes the steaks, and we have a steak fry.

THE END OF SCHOOL and the advent of summer are welcomed in our family. Mother plans and organizes cleaning assignments, and we all work together. Three girls and Mother take turns reading aloud and working. This works well when a job is concentrated in one room, like washing walls and ceilings, cleaning cabinets, making draperies, and so on. We get a lot done and read a lot of good books in the process.

WHENEVER WE HAVE SEWING PROJECTS, we all work together, assembly-line fashion. One person runs the sewing machine; another one cuts, pins, and bastes; and another presses. Depending on how many are participating, we divide up the jobs. The work gets done fast, and we all have fun working together.

WE HAVE A FAMILY GARDEN in the summer, and each of us has a section to tend. The rule is, if you don't work, you don't eat. We sing a lot together as we work. One of our favorites is a Primary song, "When We're Helping." At harvest time we make extra money by selling some of our produce.

EVERY FALL our family goes to some potato fields in Idaho to pick up potatoes after the big machines have harvested them. We always take a big picnic lunch and enjoy the splendor of the fall colors. We each pick up two sacks of potatoes, which we take home to share with friends and relatives. We put some of the sacks in a hole in the ground and cover them with straw and wood to keep them over the winter for our own use.

QUILTING IS A TRADITION in our family. Every Thanksgiving vacation we tie a quilt for every member of the family. We watch for sales so we'll have plenty of material on hand. We teach the children how to tie quilts, and once in a while we do a quilted quilt. We use the quilts for our own beds, for our trousseaus, and for gifts for friends. We all have a great time telling stories around the quilt. Then later we all help bind the quilts while we watch TV.

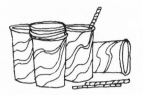

ONE COUPLE LOVE TO ENTERTAIN, and their guests can tell. They have made it a custom to involve their guests as much as they can. This makes the work a part of the party. After one of their delicious dinners, they take bids on who will dry the glassware, the silverware, the plates, and the pots and pans. They do the washing themselves. The hostess washes the first half while the host entertains guests in the living room. Then they switch places, usually with much merriment. As each task is completed, the assisting guests return to the party. One of the big advantages is that since washing dishes requires very little attention from the brain, the dishwashing team can share special times on a one-to-one basis, which doesn't often happen at a party. Sometimes the most fun takes place in the kitchen.

WE TRY TO FOSTER the attitude that problems aren't undesirable or bad; rather, they are intriguing, like a riddle. They are a challenge to our creative ability and are necessary for our growth. When we have problems, we make it a game. How can we state the problem best? This is important, because a problem well-stated is often half solved. When the problem is properly stated and agreed upon, we contribute as many alternatives as we can think of, whether they sound plausible or not. Then we start narrowing down the alternatives. The more we narrow them down, the nearer we get to the solution. And the more participation we engender in the solution, the more family members are dedicated to making it work. Our family calls an impromptu family problem-solving session around the dining room whenever we feel the need. We do it with our dinner bell. Three long rings means "Come on—we've got a problem to solve," and family members come running to participate.

PARENTS CAN'T BE EVERYWHERE at once. Yet constant vigilance is required if we are to endow our children with our own value system and not that of TV, a neighbor, or a baby-sitter. This is particularly a challenge for the working mother or a single parent.

When Becky was little, her mother had to work. The children were told to hurry straight home from school. It was not to an empty house, though, for they always found a little treat and an envelope for each of them containing instructions on what to do before she got home from work. The children were a team, working together to help create that home. Years later, Becky is now using her mother's traditions and adding her own creative ideas to build a very successful family and career.

Becky and Ken have developed a wonderful partnership arrangement for the nurturing of their little family. She works only part-time, but the demands of her job sometimes take her away from home for several days at a time. Ken's schedule is flexible, and he takes care of the four children when he can. At other times a babysitter or grandmother helps out.

When the children were small, Becky would prepare a large manila envelope for each child, with letters and suggestions for things to do while she was away. Sometimes treats were included. Now that the children are a little older, she makes a tape for each one, to be played at breakfast each day she is away. She gives them a good start on their day with instructions, encouragement, and suggestions. Her influence is felt strongly each day she is away, and the tapes can be put away as treasured, captured memories. Sometimes the tapes are designed to inspire appreciation for a member of the family, with someone different featured each day. Sometimes, if grandmother is there, Becky tells special stories about her to help the children know her better and appreciate her more. Occasionally Becky takes one of the children with her for an adventure together.

One of the benefits in all this is that the children have learned to adjust and grow to meet different situations. Pitching in to fill the void left by their mother's absence has led to discussions of what would happen if she should die—could they get along and carry on in her absence? They all agree that her life and inspiration would continue to guide them.

The children have developed ways to surprise and please their mother when she returns from a trip. Sometimes a welcome home banner will greet her. Sometimes they insert a long sheet of paper in the typewriter and keep a log each day of what has happened while she was away. The log is rolled up and presented to her when she returns and then added to the precious box of family mementoes she is collecting.

OUR FAMILY MOTTO is "If life hands you a lemon, make lemonade." And we back it up with action. When our house burned down, we called a family council. The insurance money was not nearly enough to replace our home, but it was enough to build a swimming pool and a tennis court. On the edge of our property was a little old house that we had been renting out. One of the alternatives to rebuilding right away was that we could live in that house and wait about five years to be able to build a new one. We voted unanimously for the swimming pool and the tennis court. We hardly minded the cramped quarters in the little house. Our family decision and the sacrifices we made together paid off, and now we have the new house. The "lemonade" was great.

WE ALWAYS TAKE CARE to stress individual talents and creativity in our family. Out of this encouragement has grown a tradition for making our own birthday and special-occasion cards. Construction paper, Magic Markers, glue, tape, and other assorted materials are always on hand. Most of the cards are hastily made, but with the rush comes a real sense of spontaneous charm. Even the least artistic person in our family makes cards that quietly, comically, or poetically express a message that cannot always be spoken.

Now a commercial greeting card seldom appears in our family and friendship circles. If one does, it only takes a few homemade cards addressed to that individual before he too becomes "enlightened"—either out of a sense of retaliation or a newly kindled, family-tradition patriotism that isn't easily doused.

NAMING A NEW KITTEN OR DOG is an honored ritual at our house. Each member of the family writes his favorite choice on a small piece of paper. Then the folded slips are placed in a semicircle around the bewildered animal. The pet chooses his own name. Whichever paper it happens to sniff, paw, or otherwise indicate, that one is opened and the name thereon is immediately bestowed. Then we all have a treat to celebrate.

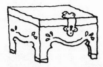

COLLECTING AND REFINISHING ANTIQUES has been a hobby that has brought us many happy, productive hours. It fosters caring about one another's wants and wishes and finding little ways to fulfill them, such as the carved, old roll-top oak desk with its import papers from England still tucked inside, my surprise for my husband; or the little doll trunk that cost too much but was worth the price to him because I loved it so. Such thoughtful caring weaves an aura of love around each antique that enhances our lives far beyond its monetary worth. Searching for things we both treasure is always an exciting adventure. Refinishing them to grace our home is very rewarding.

Making Music

Music, a powerful shaping force, can soothe or inspire, soften tensions or unify people; it can pay a tribute, teach a message, create a mood, or sell a product; it can build suspense or fear, excite to war or patriotic fervor; it can whisper a prayer or shout a hallelujah. Every producer of drama uses its creative powers to manipulate moods and feeling.

Modern science has put at our fingertips a wealth of music of all types and from all ages. It is within our power to use music to enhance and implement our own design for our family and home.

My mother's soft lullabies were my last goodnight, and my father's wake-up call, the strident tones of "Oh, how I hate to get up in the morning," dragged me reluctantly from sleep. Together they constitute some of my most precious memories. I thought Dad invented those words about murdering the bugler. It was years before I gave Irving Berlin the credit.

Music is important in a child's life, and even a simple lullaby can help open up a world of love and appreciation for music. Many of the great lessons of life can be learned from the lives of the great musicians. Pablo Casals taught his students to be free, but he also taught them that freedom is not disorder. Sibelius taught that we use the chisel of our will power to shape the granite of our lives into the design we choose. He stressed that it is as important to have a design as it is to have a sharp chisel.

Sesame Street has taught us all how music can be used to teach and reinforce concepts. Many successful parents use music and the lives of musicians as effective teaching tools.

MUSIC HAS ALWAYS been the heart of our home. It has helped to give us a love of beauty, and we've learned that one does not have to possess beauty to enjoy it. Now that I'm grown, I can better appreciate the way our parents chose to introduce us to the masters through the background music that permeated our home. They told us fascinating stories too, about the lives of Mozart, Beethoven, Bach, and many other great composers. We grew up loving many kinds of music.

IT IS TRADITIONAL in our family to try to find a creative approach to the problems that arise. Some time ago we were dis-

turbed by the quarreling and whining of our children, so we put
the tape recorder out and recorded the discord.

One night we called all the family into the living room and
played a few phrases of many kinds of music—the waltz, soft
rock, jazz, country, and so forth—and told everyone to do
whatever the music made them feel like doing. We all joined in
and frolicked together in improvised movements of dance.

Then we said, "We make different kinds of music in our
home, our own symphony of sound. Let's listen to some of the
music our family creates and see what it makes us feel like
doing." We flipped on the tape recorder and watched the ex-
pressions on their faces as they listened to themselves and felt
the jar of discordant tones and words. It was easy then to talk
about the kind of tone and rhythm we would like our family to
have. Everyone wanted to help our family sing a different song.

MOTHER TAUGHT US to use hymns with their beautiful
messages to strengthen our lives. In difficult moments a whole
hymn could play through our minds or send a prayer heaven-
ward without a note being sung out loud.

ALL THE CHILDREN IN OUR FAMILY start piano lessons at
the age of eight, and as soon as they are in junior high school,
they are encouraged to start learning another instrument of
their choice. Music teaches discipline. Being a part of a band or
orchestra is excellent training.

WE WERE SHORT OF FUNDS for music lessons, so we decided that since we could afford enough for only one child to
take lessons, that child would take the lessons and then teach

everyone else in the family. It's amazing how the teacher learns more than students do. Our "teacher's" teacher was astounded at her progress. And we all learned to play the piano.

WHEN A CHILD TURNS TWELVE at our house, he or she becomes the official song leader for family home evenings and special occasions, and serves until the next child is twelve. Dad helps us learn to conduct, and we become familiar with time and rhythm.

PARENTS CAN HELP CHILDREN find enjoyment in music with good records at story time, musical games, rhythm instruments, and music boxes. Creating your own music is even more fun. Along with the lullabies she sang for us, Mother made up a song for each one of her eight children. Today, even though we're all grown up with families of our own, we still sing all those songs at special gatherings. We children made up songs too, for each other and for our parents.

NAME THAT TUNE became a spontaneous game at our house. Someone would hum a snatch of a tune, and everyone else would try to supply the rest. Sometimes we would just beat out rhythm. It was as challenging as solving riddles, and we were constantly trying to find a tune that no one could name.

A FAMILY TRADITION was born one year when our annual neighborhood Christmas party was coming up in only one week, and our family was again without a number for the program. At dinner one night, determined to consolidate our varied talents, we began to brainstorm ways we could all perform together. Kyle, fifteen, suggested that he could play his electric bass guitar. That brought a harumph from Dad, who reminded us all that he had played second violin in the college orchestra thirty years earlier. "In fact," he stated proudly, "I also played the string bass and the tuba in the Navy."

"Good grief," I sighed, rolling my eyes, "I suppose this means I get to play my clarinet again. I'm good, you know, but clarinets are not my favorite solo instrument. Why don't I play the piano instead?"

"What about me?" Mom said hesitantly. "Am I supposed to sing?"

"You can play the piano," Kyle said quickly. "I know you can play 'Silent Night.' I've heard you when you thought nobody was around."

That settled matters. Considering our sparse list of options, we spent little time choosing a number to perform, "Silent Night."

The first practice session was very interesting. Dad's violin cried for oil like a squeaky door; Mom was a little too creative with her eighth notes; and Kyle needed less amplification. My clarinet blended fairly well, except for the few times I forgot to transpose the notes in the hymnbook to the key of B-flat. Nevertheless, as the afternoon wore on, each note found a comfortable spot that seemed to trouble the ears less and less.

The big day came and guests arrived at our home for the celebration. As the program began, we cast apprehensive glances at one another. A beautiful violin solo brought sighs from the group, and one mother read a moving Christmas story. At last we could squirm in our seats no longer; our turn had come. As we opened our respective instrument cases and hauled out the music stands, members of our audience spoke quietly to one another.

"I didn't know Helen could play the piano."

"A bass guitar—imagine that."

"Why haven't we heard this combination before?"

With shaky faith we began our song, and as it flowed from our fingers, something took those squeaky tones and dressed them in robes of family love and the spirit of new tradition. Glancing at one another and smiling broadly, we opened up and confidently played those immortal notes, "All is calm, all is bright . . ."

DAD STARTED A TRADITION by demonstrating different sounds made when one blows into bottles filled with various levels of water. We each tried playing very simple tunes just for fun. After dinner we'd get out our bottles and tune up. Then we got a bit more sophisticated and added a tub string bass, made out of an upside-down tub with a broom handle against the side of the tub and a string from the broom handle to the middle of the tub. A lot of clowning went with our act. Soon we were being asked to perform at special functions at school and in the community. Our bottle band kept our teen years so busy, we didn't have time to stray.

WHILE MAKING CHRISTMAS COOKIES one day, we realized that we were doing something we didn't really enjoy and weren't particularly good at. Yet we wanted to share something from our family with neighbors and friends. As we talked it over, we realized that what we did love and were really good at was music. We decided to leave the goodies to others and to give our music to those around us. We polished up our singing, accompanied it with bells and triangles, and set the mood with decorated lanterns. Never have we done anything so rewarding. Each year we present programs not only for neighbors and friends, but for shut-ins and other groups as well.

A GROUP OF YOUNG SINGERS practiced their carols with harp accompaniment. The effect was so lovely that they took the harp with them when they caroled on a street corner downtown. They attracted a great deal of attention, and the concert became a yearly tradition.

Traveling

Traveling is often very difficult for children. The long hours can be very tedious and boring. Adults usually love to escape from everyday demands and schedules, but for children, traveling can be a seemingly endless endurance test. Often they become so restless that it's an ordeal for parents to take them along. Some parents give up and don't ever take the children. For others a trip becomes a nightmare of cross words and quarreling. The problems can be solved with creative traditions that make traveling exciting for every age. Here are some that have proved effective.

PLANNING AND ANTICIPATION are half the fun of any trip, so we start planning early. We have a tradition that we never go in debt for a trip. We all decide how we can save enough to pay for it. Everyone helps, even the little ones. We write for articles and brochures from the area we plan to visit and spend weeks researching and planning, considering little side trips and special events. Later, when we come home, we make a scrapbook with everyone contributing.

WHEN OUR FAMILY TRAVELS we always get a "headlight start." We all tumble out of bed excited and eager to watch the sun come up and a strange new landscape come to life as we drive through the predawn hours. Sometimes we are rewarded with a magnificent display of color across the sky. This, one of the greatest masterpieces of nature, often fades unseen by the eyes of a sleeping world.

WHEN SOMEONE TRAVELS and leaves our family circle, Mother writes a special letter to that person. The letter, a personal note of praise, love, and appreciation, is tucked deep into the suitcase where the loved one will find it a day or so later. This tradition brightens up what might otherwise be a lonely journey, or if it is an exciting pleasure trip, the influence of the family reaches out to share love.

A "HAPPY TRAVEL BOX" is given to our friends and family members who travel. Directions are given inside the box on when to open certain surprises that enliven each part of the trip. They might read "You can create this when you see a brown cow" or "Open only after singing ten songs" or "Proceed to card number three only after you have bestowed a kiss upon a favorite relative." The box is filled with letters, books, games, and goodies. *Bon voyage* is scrawled in different languages all over the box.

OUR FAVORITE GAME for long trips is "King or Queen for a Day." Everybody gets a turn. If there aren't enough days during the trip for each person to be honored, we sometimes do it for half days or even hours. The person who is king (or queen) gets to choose where he sits in the car, and everyone plays his favorite activities and sings his favorite songs. We tell favorite stories about the honored person and try to make him feel like a king.

A HAPPY MEMORY of my childhood will always be the tradition of singing songs on family car trips. I can still remember my disappointment when my older brothers and sisters were "too old" to sing kids' songs. Songs like "Horsey, Horsey," "White Coral Bells," and "I've Been Working on the Railroad" still strike a tender spot in my heart.

WHEN WE TRAVEL, we sing songs that our grandmother taught us. They are age-old favorites handed down through the years by her mother and her grandmother. Sometimes we meet

new relatives and laugh together because they know the same
silly songs.

$ $$$$$$$$$

A REVERSE REWARD SYSTEM enlivened our family trips. At
the beginning of the trip, we were each given ten dimes. They
were a gift with no strings attached except that anytime quar-
rels or cross words were heard, those involved had to forfeit a
dime to Mother. A prize was given to the person with the most
dimes left when we arrived at our destination.

WE USED OUR TRAVEL TIME for sharing jokes, stories, and
special feelings. It's a shame to miss the powerful opportunity of
a captive audience when there is so little time to share. Our
parents told many stories about their childhood and their parents' pioneer experiences. We never tired of tales about "when
I was a little boy or little girl." Sometimes we took turns telling
our favorite experience from a previous trip we had taken.

OUR FAMILY TRIP BOOK is a treasure. It dates back to when
our parents were first married and tells about their honeymoon
trip. Mother has added a little write-up on each trip we've
taken since then, including the dates, places visited, highlights
of the trip, interesting things that happened, and the mode of
travel. The book brings back memories of special moments in
our family history.

WE READ BOOKS when we travel by car. Mother usually does the reading, and she chooses something that will interest everyone. Sometimes we'll complete an entire book. Of course, we take time out for snacks and naps and just relaxing, but we love to listen to stories about the places we are going. Once on a month-long camping trip through the eastern United States, we read a book on early American history. Places like Boston, Jamestown, and Fredericksburg really came to life when we saw them and read about them at the same time.

MOTHER MADE A SEAT COVER that fit over the back of the front seat. On the back-seat side were eight big pockets. When we went on a trip, five of the pockets were filled with crayons and coloring books, games, riddles, and treats. Sometimes they were sealed with pins, and little notes indicated what time they could be opened. The other three pockets were labeled with our names and were to be used to keep our clutter in. Whenever a trip was announced, we could hardly wait to tie the bulging seat cover in place and be on our way. It kept us happy and content for hours and the car tidy and neat.

UPON RETURNING HOME, a member of our family who has been away can expect to find a beautiful flower in a bud vase in his or her room. The symbol conveys the traditional message, "We love you, we missed you, and we're glad you are back."

WHEN DAD WOULD ANNOUNCE, "Now don't plan any-thing for Friday night and Saturday—we're going on an over-nighter," it was a cue for an exciting week of anticipation and planning. Each child would pack his own backpack, which Dad would inspect on Thursday night. After school on Friday, we were off. We would drive into the nearby hills, leave the car in a convenient spot away from the road, and head into the woods for no place in particular. We learned to love the outdoors, the smell of the woods, the rustle of the leaves underfoot, the sound of a rushing stream, the warmth of the campfire, and the taste of squaw bread hot from the fire. But best of all was the love we shared under the stars. Then, rejuvenated, we'd return home Saturday night.

OUR FAMILY IS LARGE, so we use a buddy system to share re-sponsibilities and make a trip more enjoyable for everyone. Each of the four older children is buddy to one of the four small-er ones. That means the older ones look out for the younger ones and help them dress, bathe, prepare for bed, and so forth. If we are camping or hiking, they help them along the trail, help carry their gear, and help them solve whatever problems come along. Self-esteem grows in both the helper, because he is needed and looked up to, and the one who is helped, who en-joys basking in the attention of a big brother or sister.

ONE OF OUR TRADITIONS grew out of something we did to fill a need. As a young married couple, we were faced with a broken-down car and no funds to fix it, so we borrowed two bicycles from our parents to get around. We had so much fun bike riding that it became a relationship-building tradition for us. As the children came along, they went too, first in baskets and later on their own bikes. I made matching sweat suits for everyone. Sometimes we put our bikes in the back of a truck and drove to a distant area to ride our bikes. Not only did we build our muscles and improve our health, but we also built strong bonds of love and sharing and respect for the world around us. We also had an incentive for getting work done quickly to leave time for the family bike ride. Somehow a bike ride together cleared the air, and feelings of dissension or resentment seemed to melt away with the whirring wheels of our bikes.

OUTFITTING THE CHILDREN for school each year was an ordeal until we made a special occasion of it. We planned a weekend trip to the closest big city. Wardrobe needs and budget allowances were discussed ahead of time so that each child knew what he could spend and what were his most important priorities. If we needed to match things, we took color swatches. Special treats, when shopping was done, were to visit the zoo or go to a movie. This became an annual tradition that no one in our family ever wanted to miss.

BUSINESS COMMITMENTS, poor health, and lack of funds have kept us from traveling as much as we hoped we could, so we decided to be arm-chair travelers. We can go any place in the world on our own "magic carpet" of books, pictures, films, and magazines. We get lots of ideas and information from *National Geographic*. Sometimes local libraries or museums have displays that add to our adventures. We've been everywhere!

MINITRIPS CAN BE FUN. Here are some ideas to consider for things that can be done in a day or two.

1. Visit the zoo.

2. Go on a picnic to a park, campground, or beach.

3. Go waterskiing.

4. Drive to a nearby city for shopping or to visit places of interest.

5. Go hiking in the country.

6. Visit an airport and watch the planes landing and taking off.

7. Explore a cave.

8. Rent motorcycles and learn to ride them.

9. Visit friends and relatives whom you don't often see.

10. Make arrangements to take a tour of a factory.

11. Hunt for minerals.

12. Go fishing.

13. Look for wildflowers and sketch them.

14. Go bird watching.

15. Visit a mining town.

16. Attend a county or state fair.

17. Visit a planetarium and see a star show.

18. Rent tandem bikes and go exploring.

19. Have a log-rolling contest at a river or lake.

20. If there's snow on the ground, go sleighriding or snowshoeing.

21. Decorate a tree for Christmas and leave it out for the animals or other passers-by to enjoy.

22. Take a bus or train ride to a nearby city.

23. Visit your state capital. If the legislature is in session, watch the proceedings.

24. Visit a courthouse and, if possible, watch a trial in session.

25. Invite friends who have traveled to bring their slides to your home for an evening of "armchair" traveling.

26. Fly kites.

27. Go for a penny walk. At each intersection, flip a coin to determine which way you will go next.

28. Rent a cabin for a night away from home.

29. Try a survival weekend trip.

30. Visit a national or state park.

31. Visit a historical monument.

32. Visit a museum or some art galleries.

33. Pan for gold in a nearby creek.

34. Inflate inner tubes and float down a river.

35. Explore walking trails.

Use your imagination. There are probably many different kinds of outings that would appeal to your family within the radius of a hundred miles or less from your home. Contact local chambers of commerce and travel bureaus for brochures.

TRAVELING, ESPECIALLY CAMPING TRIPS, can be more enjoyable if you plan ahead. Here are some suggestions for your next outing:

Pack lightly—who cares if you wear the same thing twice?

Don't bog yourselves down with nonessentials unless you know specifically that you will need them.

Have a place (preferably out of sight) for *everything* in the car. Clothes, games, toothbrushes, coloring books, crackers, and other miscellaneous items can create chaos and frustration. When a car is relatively clean and neat, things seem to run much more smoothly.

Have your car checked thoroughly before you leave. Car troubles put a damper on any vacation, especially when parts are hard to find.

Plan carefully. Don't throw everything haphazardly into the car and hope you have what you need. You'll end up with much more of some things that you need, not enough of other things, and a carload of cross people.

Have a "camping kit" prepacked with such essentials as eating utensils, dishes, salt and pepper, matches, and a can opener. Make a list of these basic items, cover it with clear Contact paper, and keep it in the glove compartment of your car. Check them off as you pack.

Take along a good map. Let family members learn how to read it and make decisions on your itinerary.

New Beginnings

Births, marriages, and deaths, the most dramatic and compelling events of life, are surrounded with traditions in every culture. In early times they were often complicated and impressive, and their main purpose was to make public and intensify the importance of the event. Even today, though the customs and traditions are usually more simplified, the purpose is the same.

WHEN WEDDINGS BRING NEW MEMBERS into our family, they are honored at a family dinner and formally ushered into the "Society of the Appendages." We initiate them into family jokes and practices and properly impress them with the wonderful family they have joined. We shower them with poems, suggestions, and advice on how to achieve success as members of our family. Then we turn the limelight on them and learn all we can about their background, hopes, dreams, and plans. Before the evening is over they belong, and an "Appendage" certificate is proudly presented to them for display in their homes.

NEW MEMBERS OF OUR FAMILY were initiated into our Family T-shirt Club with a water fight. Usually it takes place a week or two before the wedding. But if it is a winter wedding, we do it on the first family outing in the spring. Each of us wears a navy blue T-shirt with our family name across the front in white letters, and our social security number across the back. After we present the new member with his T-shirt, the water fight begins. We don't stop until everyone is soaked. After one good water fight, the barriers are down and the new member is properly "in."

Newborn babies in our clan each receive a T-shirt with numbers 0000 on the back. But water fighting for them waits until they are big enough to splash and join the fun.

A FAMILY HOME EVENING is held in our family a day or two before the wedding with family members from far and near attending. We honor the bridal couple and express love and appreciation to them. It is a night of remembering and featuring special events in their lives and expressing tender feelings. The evening ends with special counsel and blessings from the parents.

QUILTING IS A TREASURED TRADITION in our family. Mother always kept a quilt on the frame. It hung from the beams of our house on a pulley system ingeniously designed by Dad. When other chores were done and there was time to quilt, the frame was lowered, and all available pairs of hands stitched away. As space was needed for other things, it was hoisted aloft again to serve as a decorative canopy. When a quilt was completed, another one replaced it, and the creation of a new treasure was begun. When anyone in the family married, the quilt chests were opened and the new home was stocked.

GRANDMOTHER MAKES BEAUTIFUL QUILTS. Some have won sweepstakes in the fairs. When there is a wedding in our family, the bride may go to Grandmother's house and pick out any quilt she wants.

WHEN THE GIRLS in our family are very young, they choose a favorite color and "register" it with Grandmother. Throughout the years she makes hope chest gifts for special occasions in each girl's favorite color, and by the time the girls are sixteen, their hope chests are filled with Grandmother's lovely gifts.

FOR BRIDES IN OUR FAMILY, someone draws pictures on quilt blocks of special events in the young woman's life. Family members and friends each take one block and embroider it. Then the quilt blocks are sewn together, and we have a quilting party. The quilt is always beautiful and a real keepsake. One of the prettiest ones was done all in a cream color. It made a gorgeous bedspread.

WHEN THERE IS A WEDDING in our family, Mother takes her favorite apron, cuts off the strings, and sends them to the spouse of her child. There they are displayed on the bulletin board or framed and hung on the wall.

A HOPE CHEST is given to each girl in our family when she graduates from high school. We have a tradition that female friends and cousins always give each other gifts for the hope chest. Grandmother gives each of us a silver spoon on our birthdays until we have a set.

HAVING A BABY is one of life's most profound events. Its importance is accented by joyful family rituals that can enhance the arrival and make the transition easier for everyone. The maternal grandmother often has the privilege of helping her daughter and new grandchild when they return from the hospital. This is a wonderful and joyful time for drawing close and sharing feelings and memories, as well as planning for the future.

We always weigh new babies in our family on Mother's candy scale, an old black balance scale with eight pounds of weights. When the baby exceeds that weight, we keep on weighing him or her by adding objects of absolute weight, such as a pound of butter. Then we take a picture of the infant balanced with the strange assortments of counterweight.

OUR GRANDPARENTS buy for the new baby a mint set of uncirculated coins of each denomination dated with the year of the child's birth. This becomes quite valuable as the years go by. (A variation of this tradition is to give first-day issues of commemorative stamps.)

GRANDMOTHER SAVES the front page of the newspaper on the day of birth, and it is put in the child's scrapbook.

OUR GRANDMOTHER MADE A COLLAGE of treasures and mementos kept since her daughter's birth and presented it to her daughter at the birth of the daughter's first child.

DURING THE LAST MONTH of a pregnancy in our family, friends and relatives make a guess as to the baby's weight, record their guesses on slips of paper, and drop them in a bottle. Sometimes we also guess the birthdate and hour. Grandfather awards a prize of twenty dollars to whoever makes the closest guess.

ALL BABIES BORN in our clan are christened in a Scottish tartan and brooch. The heirlooms are passed down through the line of the oldest son but made available for each new baby.

GRANDMOTHER PREPARES a looseleaf binder for each new baby in the family, filling it with the favorite songs and stories of the family. This keeps memories of all our family favorites alive.

FROM THE HOSPITAL after the birth of each of her children, Mother always wrote a beautiful letter to each of us children at home, telling about the new baby and of Mother's love for us. This helped prepare the way for the new baby's homecoming.

THE DAY WE DISCOVERED we were going to have a baby, I started a letter to him, telling of our joy and excitement over his coming. It was an ongoing letter to which I added details about the interesting special thoughts and feelings, hopes and desires. After he was born, I wrote about his birth.

This letter was the beginning of his diary that I kept for him until he was big enough to do it for himself. Once a week, while he was small, I printed for him the good and bad things of that week. Along the margins I added my own thoughts and explanations in cursive. When he was old enough to write for himself, he continued his story. We've extended this tradition to each new arrival in the family.

ON THE BIRTHDAY OF EACH CHILD, after the party is over and presents have been opened, we have a quiet time of reminiscence. I have kept a diary for twenty-two years, and I find the pages that describe the birth of the child. I read it aloud— our preparation for the event, all the happenings of that day, going to the hospital, the description of the birth, and our feelings about it. Then we read the child's diary, which I have kept, telling the general events in his lifetime and especially the amusing things he has said. We all enjoy this very much and it gives the child a sense of his origins and continuity.

THE NAMING OF A CHILD has important significance in many cultures. Great care should be taken in the choosing of a name. As Evelyn Wells says in *What to Name the Baby*, "My name is my representative force in the hearing of those who make up my world, my sound effect, my story and my theme song, my personal share in the moving history of the land!" She adds, "A fitting and high sounding name is the best gift you can give to the newly born for it will be his to live with all his life and it may in itself hold the success or failure of that future."

Family tradition has always figured prominently in the naming of children. The ancient Greeks made a hereditary chain of naming every other son after his grandfather. Many children today are still named for parents and grandparents. Problems and confusion can sometimes be avoided by using different middle names.

The Bateman family for generations gave the oldest son the first name of James. We broke the five-generation tradition partly because my husband had never been fond of James as a name and partly because we weren't aware of its importance to the family. We lived far away from relatives who might have influenced us. We have always been a little sorry about that. One of the important ideas we should convey to children is to honor and appreciate their name, to know its history, and to take pride in it.

Many families honor the mother by giving each child her surname as a middle name. Others use just the initial. Care should be taken that neither the name nor the initials formed suggest a nickname that might be detrimental to the child's self-concept or personality. Nicknames can express endearment, affection, and an intimate feeling of belonging or sometimes just be fun and descriptive.

Kyle Eric Jam Ice Cream Bateman lives at our house, but he wasn't born with that distinguished title. It all began with the threat of rheumatic fever. The doctor decreed, "I believe it is a very mild case. With lots of rest, limited exertion, and plenty of good food to put some meat on that spindly body, we'll nip this in the bud."

Mom went to work on the food plan: after school, a peanut butter and jam sandwich; two hours later, dinner with second helpings and dessert, usually a heaping bowl of vanilla ice cream. Gradually the threat of rheumatic fever lessened and disappeared.

Years have passed and the schedule has faded, but the jam and mountainous bowls of ice cream remain. Kyle munches his traditional snacks during breakfast, before lunch, after his walk home from school, and between TV shows. The food plan never did fatten him up, but Kyle Eric Jam Ice Cream Bateman made a name for himself that just won't quit—at least, not until he quits living up to it.

Red Letter Days

Birthdays

MY BIRTHDAY is a celebration of my life. It is mine! Probably no other day of the year has the same potential for the deliberate enhancement of a person's sense of self-worth and his awareness that others value him too.

A few years ago, about the time Dr. Seuss first published his *Birthday Book*, a group of dear friends got together and celebrated each others' birthdays. What a joy it was to meet for lunch with friends who went to special effort to create for us a memorable birthday. I'll never forget my "Dr. Seuss Party." Three of us had birthdays the same week, so the party honored all three. The hostesses for the day made all the clever trappings from Dr. Seuss: the birthday horn, the birthday bird (with an eight-foot wingspread made of chicken wire and crepe paper), the tallest of the "allest" (about nine feet high), the Smorgasboard. We drove to the top of a tall peak and shouted to the sky, "I am what I am and I'm glad that I am, that I'm not just a dish of sour gooseberry jam." Then we played the crazy instruments they provided and formed a band made of "plumbers that plumb as they come and zummers that zum as they come."

We were giddier and gayer than our own children and went home buoyed up in spirit and love, ready to tackle another year of being the rock of Gibraltar for everyone else in the family.

I was so impressed with the *Birthday Book* message of "celebrating me" and "believing in me" that I borrowed all the props and reenacted it for our son, who was suffering a bad case of teenage "everything's-the-matter-with-me woes." It worked. I've used that book ever since in all my classes when I teach about self-image. It says so well "You are who you are. Now isn't that *great!*"

BIRTHDAYS IN OUR HOME are not simple affairs. Only one thing happens the same every birthday: our traditional "bad kid" routine. Just before the official birthday meal, the gifts are stored in one room. Dad gathers the family around the table and we begin. Prayer is said, and then Dad orders all the "bad kids" out of the room. All of the children except the birthday person march out of the kitchen to the room where the gifts are. After taping cards on the packages, straightening ribbons, and dividing the gifts, the "bad kids" beg to return to the table. After promising future good behavior, they are allowed to return. We all sing "Happy Birthday," and the presents are laid at the special person's place. This ceremony has made birthdays seem special. The few minutes the birthday child spends alone with Dad, laughing and joking, while the "bad kids" are out, helps forge a special alliance.

THE REAL TREAT on birthdays at our house is when Dad takes the birthday person out sometime during the preceding week to pick out a present, go to dinner (where the waitresses always sing "Happy Birthday" and present a small cake with sparklers in the center), and then go to a movie. A night out with Dad is so special that each of us looks forward to it all year.

MY MOTHER keeps a file folder on each one of us. On our birthdays she makes a kind of bulletin board in the kitchen where all can see. It spotlights the birthday person and what he or she has done all year. This makes each of us feel honored and proud.

BIRTHDAY WAKE-UP at our house is a real production. All the family troops to the birthday person's room, and each of us pulls on his earlobes gently, the number of times of his age and one to grow on. There are kisses and hugs and "happy birthdays," and then he is led blindfolded to the table. Serpentine falls from the chandelier and balloons are everywhere. His place is always piled with presents. Then we light the cake—a big, hot, butter-pecan coffee cake. When the blindfold comes off, he sees the cake ablaze and all the smiling family. It is worth getting up an hour early for a birthday like that. The birthday posters stay on the wall the whole day to remind him how much he is loved and appreciated.

FOR EVERY BIRTHDAY PERSON our family makes a long birthday card that covers the dining room wall. Everybody helps, and we make it very colorful with pictures, messages, and jokes from all of us.

WE DECORATE the birthday person's room and hang a crepe-paper canopy over his bed while he sleeps. A trail of balloons leads to where a present is hidden. Then we bang on pots and pans to wake the person up.

OUR FAMILY GOES SHOPPING together occasionally to buy some piece of matching clothing—usually sweat shirts, shirts, or hats. Then on birthdays and other special occasions we all wear these matching clothes.

DECEMBER BIRTHDAYS are always a challenge because of the pressures of Christmas preparations. One year our daughter's cake didn't get frosted in time for her party. Undaunted, I passed out aprons to all the little guests and let them design and help decorate the cake. We made it into a little house ready for Christmas, complete with Santa's sleigh and reindeer. The games we had planned could not possibly have been as much fun. That stands out as one of our most memorable birthdays. Another birthday party I didn't have time to prepare for featured an impromptu taffy pull.

OUR BIRTHDAY PERSON gets to choose which kind of cake he wants. We have a whole book of possibilities, everything from turtles to old witches. When we were little, we would pour over the book for weeks before our birthdays while we tried to decide.

MOTHER PUTS TOOTHPICKS in the cake to keep the layers from sliding, and whoever gets a toothpick can make a wish. One of the things we look forward to the most is the extra cake she always bakes and invites the neighbors to share the day after the birthday.

NO ONE AT OUR HOUSE likes cake very much, so we always have a birthday pie, complete with candles. The birthday person chooses the kind of pie we'll have.

EACH CHILD IN OUR FAMILY has a tall birthday candle with eighteen little marks, one for each year. It occupies the center of our table for each birthday. Every year we burn the candle down to the next mark, a kind of advent to adulthood. By the eighteenth birthday, it has burned away.

BIRTHDAY MEALS usually consist of the favorite foods of the birthday person, but they can be varied in many ways:

1. Have hot apple sauce on ice cream for breakfast.
2. Serve breakfast in bed to the birthday person.
3. Have a special midnight snack.
4. Let the birthday person choose where to go to dinner.
5. Sit around the table holding hands while singing "Happy Birthday."
6. Let the birthday person choose the food for all three meals.
7. Let the birthday person sit in Dad's place at the dinner table.

IN THE EARLY YEARS when our family didn't have much money, we had cooked cereal every morning. Mother always scrubbed and polished pennies, nickels, and dimes, and put them in the hot cereal as a surprise on our birthdays. Everyone got some, but the birthday person got the most.

OUR CHILDREN WERE SMALL and we were far away in Spain when we received word of the death of my mother. In deep appreciation for her, and with some regrets, I realized you can never do enough for the mother who gave you life. I started the tradition of having each child give his mother a gift on his own birthday. Gifts are also given to the birthday child, but the important thing for him is the present he prepares to give his mother in appreciation for the gift of life.

THE CHILDREN IN OUR FAMILY raise Saint Bernard dogs. As each of the children reaches the age of eight, he has the privilege of deciding what color our huge doghouse is going to be. The eight-year-old makes the decision, and then the rest of the family abides by the child's wishes by doing the actual painting. Needless to say we have had a pretty wild-looking doghouse at times. It stays that color until the next child reaches eight years of age.

IN OUR FAMILY of eight children, we have a special party when one of the children turns sixteen. It's a sort of coming-of-age party, with seventy-five guests invited. All the children, even the little ones, help plan the party.

EACH DAUGHTER in our family receives a small gold necklace in the shape of a heart, with her name engraved on it, for her sixteenth birthday. This has been a family tradition for two generations.

WE HAVE A TRADITION surrounding an old cane that has long been in the family. When any male member of the family turns fifty, we have a big family party, and his name is carved into the cane.

MOTHER AND DAD taught us that we are in charge of our own lives. They wrote a biography of each of us for our eighth birthday. Then they helped us write up our plans for the future, including school, career, and marriage. We filed these away in our own file boxes. Each year on our birthdays we take our stories and goal sheets and make changes and amendments from that year's vantage point. Our parents are always supportive and never criticize or laugh at our childish goals. But often, a year or two later, we laugh together about how much we have grown and changed. Goals we've achieved are always celebrated with praise and recognition. Then we define new ones.

IT'S A TRADITION in our family for each person on his or her birthday to write a letter to himself or herself to be opened the following year. Parents help the younger children. We always include the goals we want to achieve and how we feel about ourselves and our family, friends, school, and church. These are all kept and bound together in a folder. They make a unique birthday milestone history.

FATHER INTERVIEWS each of us on the night before our birthday and asks us how our life is progressing, how we feel about it, and what we would like to do in the coming year. We make a list of goals for the coming year. Father always tapes the interviews, and those tapes are some of our most treasured possessions.

WE HAVE AN ANNUAL HOUSE BIRTHDAY. We were so thrilled when we finally moved into our new home that we decided to celebrate the anniversary of that date every year with a spruce-up time. We have a family planning meeting about a month ahead and decide what needs to be done. Sometimes we also have an open house on the anniversary and invite friends and neighbors. One of the most anticipated things is the special gift we buy each year for our home. We plan ahead and save for it, and the whole family participates in the planning and saving. Some of the nicest things we own are birthday presents we bought for our home.

KEEPING UP WITH BIRTHDAYS of extended family members—aunts, uncles, cousins—is often difficult. In order to keep our relationships growing, we chose a month when there were no birthdays in our immediate family and made a birthday gift box to mail to one of the extended families. The gift was so appreciated that we've continued the tradition with other distant relatives. Sometimes we include little gifts for each person in the family with a note or card wishing each one happy birthday. Sometimes we choose a family gift, such as a box of cheese. We always include letters or tape recordings. This tradition of love and sharing keeps our families close and in touch with one another.

New Year's

New Year's is a time of contrasts, a time for treasuring memories and defining new goals. It is a time to contemplate and a time to celebrate. It is an end and a beginning.

I was invited once to share the vassilopitta ceremony with a Greek family. Vassilopitta is a large cake (about twelve to fourteen inches in diameter) flavored with lemon and decorated with numbers representing the New Year plus assorted greetings. The cake is placed before the host, who traces a cross in the air above it with his knife and then cuts the first piece, puts it on a plate, and names it for Jesus. He names the second piece for the house, the third for the master, then the mistress, each of the children from the oldest to the youngest, guests, and family members not present. A silver coin has been baked in the cake, and whoever receives it will be lucky throughout the year. If, after all persons present have eaten their cake, the coin has not been found, the other pieces are each probed with a fork. When the coin is found, it is sent to the person for whom that piece has been named, with a letter of congratulations for his good fortune and blessing for the coming year.

TO CELEBRATE THE NEW YEAR, many people eat foods that are special to them. One family enjoys oyster stew by candlelight on New Year's Eve, a family tradition for three generations. Another family always has dinner featuring ham on New Year's Day; then they all go ice skating together. Breakfast at a grandmother's house is one family's tradition, with finnan haddie and scones and jam on the menu. Since their father's birthday comes on New Year's Eve, another family celebrates with his favorite cuisine—Italian.

NEW YEAR'S EVE FOODS at our home always include eggnog, shrimp, and chips and dips. At 11:59 P.M. the New Year is announced by every noise-producing object in the house. Timers are set, alarm clocks buzz, instruments are played, and everyone adds his part by cheering. The lucky person who found the Thanksgiving turkey's wishbone chooses a partner, makes a wish, and breaks the bone.

OUR FAMILY goes to the *Nutcracker* ballet on New Year's Eve. Every Christmas Santa leaves the tickets in our stockings. Then we say good-bye to the holiday season by breaking up our gingerbread house just as the clock strikes twelve.

WE DISCUSS OUR FAMILY GOALS on New Year's Eve and choose three we can all work on for the coming year. Usually a goal is selected in each of three areas: recreational (vacations, hobbies, and sports); spiritual (scripture reading, serving others); home improvement (redecorating our rooms, remodeling, refurbishing, and so forth).

NEW YEAR'S EVE is a night for memories. We show all our slides and pictures of the past year, and laugh and cry at the good times and the bad. We also take a family group picture that night.

WE SPEND NEW YEAR'S DAY writing about significant happenings of the past year. Then we combine our contributions into a family history. We also work on scrapbooks and photo albums and bring them up-to-date.

NEW YEAR'S DAY is take-the-Christmas-tree-down day. As we put away the treasured ornaments, we contemplate the past year and make plans for the new one. Each of the children makes a list of the things he wants for the coming year and puts it in his Christmas stocking before the stockings are packed away. Then at Christmas when the stockings are taken out to be hung once again, we enjoy reading the notes and seeing whether the year has brought fulfillment of the children's desires.

ON THE MONDAY after New Year's, each of us opens our last year's resolutions. We keep them in a "time bomb" that Mother puts away until the next year. After the old resolutions are read and discussed, we choose new ones and seal them up. We try to make resolutions that will improve family and home life.

Valentine's Day

MOM IS A "VALENTINE LADY" on February 14. After supper that night, she puts on a big apron and gathers it up like a basket, then fills it with candies and tiny presents. We follow her in a dance through the house. At the end of the dance, she lets her apron go, and we scramble for the treats. We also make brownies, and everyone gets a big piece with his name on it.

ON VALENTINE'S DAY we give each other some type of candy—perhaps just a mint. Just before dinner we place our offering by each plate, and then Mother puts boxes of heart candy and a lot of other little things under our plates and turns them over so we can't see the goodies. After the blessing on the food, we lift the plates up to see what treasures we can find.

MOM PUTS A LITTLE PRESENT beside each plate, and she also decorates the kitchen with hearts and flowers. Dad buys my sister, my mother, and me each a beautiful flower and a card that expresses his feelings of love toward his sweethearts.

MAMMOTH SUGAR COOKIES decorated with our names and messages of love are Mother's valentine to us. She hides each person's cookie in a place where it is sure to be discovered.

VALENTINE'S DAY TRIMMINGS of red, pink, and white paper and white lace are put on the breakfast table, and everyone makes "Luv U" cards. These special valentines are always cherished and saved.

WAKE-UP TIME on Valentine's Day means a personal visit from Mom and Dad with big hugs and kisses. We bake valentine cookies to take to friends and neighbors. We leave them at each door, then ring the bell and run. Our friends are doing the same thing, so doorbells are ringing all evening around our area.

Presidents' Birthdays

We proudly fly our nation's flag every national holiday and teach our children to honor and respect it. On Lincoln's birthday we serve a chocolate dessert log for dinner and review some of the stories of his life.

WASHINGTON'S BIRTHDAY is observed at our house with a big cherry cake. Tucked here and there in the cake are tiny gifts wrapped in plastic, and above each of them, a little American flag marks the spot. Sometimes if the gifts are personalized, Mother writes a name on the flag. Then each of us tells a story we enjoy about Washington. Dad always comes up with a new one we haven't heard before.

Easter

SINCE THE CHILDREN are out of school at Eastertime, we like to take short trips in our camper. We color hard-cooked eggs before we leave, and we take along empty Easter baskets. On Friday night, while the children are sleeping, we hide eggs all around the inside of the camper. In addition to the eggs, we hide picnic foods, each wrapped in a different color. Besides finding the Easter eggs, each person must find a package of each color to fill his basket. For instance, apples are wrapped in red, potato chips in yellow, canned juice in green, cupcakes in brown. Sandwiches or chicken pieces are hidden in the re-frigerator. When everyone's basket is full, we go for a hike and picnic. After such a glorious day in the beautiful, awakening-to-spring world, we are ready for a reverent Sunday.

BECAUSE EASTER is such a significant spiritual occasion, we dress in our best clothes for church and dinner that day. Mother prepares the meal on Saturday, to be warmed up on Sunday, and we set our table with our finest china and silver-ware.

ONE PERSON IN OUR FAMILY is chosen to prepare a special egg, elaborately dyed and decorated. This egg is hidden in the yard, and whoever finds it in the Easter egg hunt gets a sum of money as a prize. The prize gets bigger as the children grow up. We started with a quarter when they were little and increased the amount as they grew older.

AT OUR HOUSE the children make a huge Easter basket and hide it in the front room for their parents.

WE HIDE JELLY BEANS all over our house for a special Easter egg hunt. Each one has a cash redemption value; no one ever knows how much. The orange ones might be worth one cent, the pink twenty-five cents, and the black one dollar. We have very diligent searchers.

MOM LEAVES OUR EMPTY BASKETS on the kitchen table on Saturday morning, with a note to lead us to the first surprise. Notes at each surprise leads us to the next one until we've filled up the baskets. The notes consist of riddles that sometimes take all day to figure out.

THE SATURDAY BEFORE EASTER, all our relatives go on a picnic. The older children color and hide the eggs for the younger ones to find. Grandma conducts a race, and we run until everyone has a prize. We play softball, eat lots of good food, and enjoy an all-day outing with loved ones.

WE ALWAYS DRESS WARMLY and go on a hike and a picnic
the day before Easter. We build a fire and roast wieners. Then
we search out as many as possible of the first signs of spring, the
rebirth and reawakening of the world after a long winter.

The Fourth of July

The biggest birthday party of the year reminds us with a
bang of the birth of America's independence. Families all over
the country have unique ways of celebrating.

Our town celebrates from the flag-raising at dawn till the
last fireworks display in the evening. "I am an American" is
loudly proclaimed from the parade floats and bunting-draped
speaker's stands, as well as by little children waving flags. It is a
day for unabashed patriotism. But it is also a family day.

Our neighbors have their most rousing celebration of the
year, and an invitation to their home on that day is highly
prized. Children and grandchildren all flock home for the traditional festivities. The day dawns early with strains of patriotic
hymns, played by the church band from the back of an enor-
mous flatbed truck. Dogs bark wildly, children wave their instruments at sleepy onlookers, and the procession ends up,
shortly after six o'clock, at a flag-raising ceremony and family
pancake breakfast.

After breakfast, it's time to go to the big community parade,
which is led by a cannon that's fired every hundred yards by
young men dressed as Yankee soldiers. Shimmering floats,
beautiful queens, vintage cars, countless high school bands,
and clowns draw applause and oohs and aahs from the specta-
tors.

The family party goes into high gear at home after the
parade. If the day is hot, Dad slips out to adjust the irrigation
ditch headgate. Then everyone dons cut-offs and T-shirts and
gathers on the back lawn, which slowly fills with water.

Finally the long-awaited softball game begins. Bases are

placed at strategic low spots on the flooded lawn. Captains choose their teams as the traditional equipment is assembled. The ball is a flat old volleyball, while a broom handle serves as a bat. The batter is out if he is hit with the ball or tagged at the base by an opposing player. The games involves much sliding, diving, ducking, slipping, splashing, and squealing.

Before the grass turns to mud, the participants fall into exhausted heaps and begin staggering to the house for dry clothes and lunch.

AT OUR FAMILY PARTY on the Fourth, everyone wears red, white, and blue. Dad tells stories about proud moments in our country's history and reminds us how blessed we are to live here. Then we all help make a freezer full of ice cream.

WE CONDUCT our own flag-raising ceremony on our porch and teach our children how to honor and treat the flag.

OUR FAMILY ALL MEETS at a certain corner to watch the Fourth of July parade. Then we go to Grandma's house for a delicious chicken dinner. Balloons, lots of red, white, and blue, and games for the children add to the festivities.

Labor Day

LABOR DAY at our home is just that—a day for labor. We all put in a day of hard work—cleaning up the garden, bottling fruit, and doing other chores together. We enjoy working together in a team effort, and we accomplish a great deal as we work together.

WE ORGANIZE OUR FAMILY into clean-up teams and do spruce-up jobs around our yard or for a widow or other person in need. Then Dad takes us out for hamburgers and thick milkshakes.

Halloween

OUR BASEMENT is the scene of a haunted house or spook alley for Halloween. Dad and Mom are always there to help with the fun and keep things under control. Sometimes we invite others in the neighborhood to participate in a Halloween party. Chili is a traditional dish on that day.

WE GO "PUMPKIN CAROLING" instead of asking for treats to celebrate Halloween. We carve pumpkins and put a candle in each, then make our rounds of the neighborhood.

HALLOWEEN AT OUR HOUSE was the greatest night of the year when we were children. Mother always made a costume for each of us, and after Halloween the costumes were put into a chest and used during the rest of the year for dress-up fun. We helped plan our own costumes and were allowed to select who or what we wanted to portray. We usually changed our minds a dozen times before Mother took the scissors to the cloth.

A WEEK BEFORE HALLOWEEN, we select three families who we think need friendship, such as a new family on the block, a lonely widow, or a child who isn't accepted by others. On Halloween we visit these people and take them special treats. Then we all go out for a special treat, such as pizza or ice cream.

Thanksgiving

THANKSGIVING, one of the most American of the holidays, has a noble purpose, but we often have to move beyond stuffing ourselves with turkey in order to experience it. Filling our hearts with appreciation drives out selfishness and despair and sets us on a higher plane. We show thankfulness to God, and how better to show it than by caring for our fellowmen.

An excellent way to celebrate Thanksgiving is to choose several people who have influenced our lives for good but who have gone unthanked, and to write them letters. We might select an old high school teacher, a person who has befriended us, or someone who shared ideas that we've used successfully. One person who started this practice years ago has a file full of delightful and poignant replies that have paid him a hundred times over for the time it took to send thank-you letters.

A THANKSGIVING TIME BOMB tradition was begun out of frustration. Mom spent untold hours preparing a dinner that was gobbled up in minutes, and then everyone left. She wanted something more. The next Thanksgiving she served the appetizers and then sprung the surprise. It was a huge glass jar decorated with the family crest and the words "Time Bomb 1973."

Between each course, family members and guests were given little tasks to do: "Write about the most beautiful thing that happened to you this year." "Trace the outline of your hand, sign it, and write on the back some things you want to train your hands to do in the next three years." "Depict in pictures the things you are most thankful for today." Each one shared his efforts, and the feast stretched out all afternoon.

After dinner, we made tape recordings of songs, poems, and memories, with everyone participating. Then the jar was sealed and carefully hidden away for three years. Each year the family makes a new "time bomb" and opens the one sealed three years ago. Opening the jar and reading the contributions has become the highlight of the day.

THANKSGIVING IS A SPIRITUAL OCCASION for our family. Before we eat dinner, each member tells what he is most thankful for. Mom puts two or three beans or kernels of corn on each plate, and we contemplate our blessings and tell about them as we eat our kernels.

Seasonal

HAILING EACH NEW SEASON for its joys and fun can bring excitement and variety in our lives. In Zurich, Switzerland, people become so excited about spring that they ring it in with a festival on Easter Monday. Children lead the parade dressed in their native finery. When all the church bells ring at six o'clock, Boog, an effigy representing winter, is set ablaze. Everyone loudly applauds the death of winter and the birth of spring.

We don't usually go so far as to burn winter in effigy but many families have their own private ways of celebrating each season.

OUR FAMILY KNOWS that on the first spring day, we will get up early and vigorously attack our spring cleaning. Dad posts a list of chores on the shed door, and we can each sign up for the ones we would rather do. We usually prefer to work together and help one another until the work is done. Then we barbeque steaks for everyone. Sometimes we go to a nearby canyon, but often it is still too cold, so we settle for the backyard.

SINCE WE WERE VERY SMALL, on the first day of spring (or the weekend nearest to it), we have taken a spring hike and planted seeds along the way. We take seeds that are hardy perennials or that reseed themselves easily. Then we enjoy a picnic lunch. This is our way of saying thanks for spring and of helping Mother Nature dress up a little more each year.

ON MARCH 15 we celebrate "Tables Eve." Everyone in the family goes to the grocery store, and we each have two dollars to spend. Each person buys what he wants for dinner, and no one else can see what we have bought until we return home. Then we make a meal of whatever we've purchased. We usually laugh about some of the selections, but we also learn a good lesson in money management.

SPRING AND SUMMER unite our family as we join together to create a beautiful garden. We each have a section to plant, water, weed, and then harvest. Mother Nature writes a report card, and it's easy to learn lessons in dependability, initiative, and responsibility when the results are so obvious.

EVERY FAMILY has special things they like to do in the summer. As a child, I enjoyed best our trips to Jenny Lake near Jackson, Wyoming, not just for the magnificent scenery and boat rides across the lake, but also because of a little ritual I shared with two favorite aunts. On a little island reached by a bridge, among stately pines and solid ancient rocks, was a special rock. We'd move the rock aside and place a brand-new penny, adding to the pennies we'd placed there previous years. Then we'd reminisce about past trips and wonder how many more times we'd be able to move our secret rock and add a new penny to its store. As we carefully replaced the heavy stone, we'd each make a wish.

The last time I visited there, the island had been torn by a storm, and I was unable to find the special rock. It may still be there with its treasure of pennies, each one a memento of memories; but it is lost to me, and with it, a lovely glow from my past.

BEFORE SCHOOL STARTS in the fall, Mother takes each of us shopping and then to lunch. We call it our farewell-to-summer, get-excited-about-school day. The night before school starts, Father gives each of us a special blessing.

DEER HUNTING SEASON in our family finds the men and boys hunting out in the hills. While they're gone, all the women and girls get together for the weekend. We go out for dinner and to a drive-in movie on Friday evening, then stay up all night visiting and laughing. It's a delightful time to get to know sisters, cousins, and aunts better.

Christmas

Of all traditions, the ones linked to Christmas are probably the most cherished. Oddly, they date far back into pre-Christian times. Since the date of Christ's birth was unknown in the fourth century, when the Christian celebration was established, it was decreed that the celebration be held on the day of the old Roman feast of the birth of Sol. Other relics of pre-Christian times include the holly, mistletoe, yule log, and wassail bowl.

"I'll be home for Christmas, if only in my dreams" is a universal thought expressed in a popular song. Christmas is a time for warm love and remembering, a time to be with loved ones.

The traditions of Christmas make us feel more secure. They provide happy memories to keep us warm, to wrap around us. Once a year mankind needs to remind itself how beautiful this season is. It feels good to sit by a lighted tree, to make a holly wreath, to sing a Christmas carol, even if we don't understand how the traditions came to be.

At Christmas, we wrap ourselves in past joys through traditions. Present joys are multiplied as the family is brought together.

WE TRY TO KEEP the true spirit of Christmas all year. When we put away the crèche after Christmas, we leave the manger on the mantel and place a pile of golden straw by it. Each family member knows that preparation for Christmas takes a whole year, and the way to prepare is to fill the manger with straw. It must be done one straw at a time though, and one earns the right to put in a straw by doing a good deed unacclaimed. If the manger is not filled with good deeds done by the family during the year, then the baby Jesus will have a cold, hard bed when Christmas comes and he is once again laid in the manger. On Christmas Eve the scene is reassembled, any unused straw is scattered around, and the tiny figure of baby Jesus is laid in the manger. We all feel part of the ceremony, because we've all helped fill the manger with straw.

ARRANGING THE NATIVITY SCENE is our most important and meaningful Christmas activity. A week before Christmas we set it up in a prominent place in our front window as a reminder of the real meaning of Christmas. Then we read Luke's

account of Jesus' birth and sing carols around the fire. Early in
our marriage we made our own little nativity figures; later the
children contributed theirs. Now we have a lovely carved wood
set, but the meaning is no more powerful than that of our old
home-made one. A candle burning beside the scene reminds us
of the light brought to the world with the birth of Christ.

THE BEST PART OF CHRISTMAS is the one we give away.
Mom always finds out about a needy family, and we provide
Christmas gifts from clothes and toys to food and treats. Secrecy is essential to our project. Since we take seriously the
statement in Matthew 25:40, "Inasmuch as ye have done it
unto one of the least of these my brethren, ye have done it unto
me," we ask someone unknown to the recipients to deliver our
gifts.

WE PREPARE WISH CARDS for all our neighbors. We write
good wishes on cards and attach them to plates of treats. Then
we light a lantern and go caroling through the neighborhood.
At each door we present a plate of treats and sing a carol. Sometimes the recipients join us, and we continue on our rounds
until the whole neighborhood glows with the glory of the
Christmas season. Some years each family is asked ahead of
time to join us as we reach their house. Then we all return to
our house for a smorgasbord supper to which each family con-
tributes. These special times together have drawn our neighborhood very close.

ON DECEMBER 1, we have a family council meeting and discuss how we can best honor the Savior this year. Then we decide on our Christmas projects. One of the projects is always a

gift-of-love tree, made of green felt and hung on our kitchen door. Hidden among its gay decorations is a little pocket for each member of the family with his or her photo on the flap. Gifts of love and time, things money can't buy, are written on cards and slipped either signed or unsigned into the pockets. We each try to make at least two cards for each person, including grandparents and other visitors who will be sharing our Christmas with us.

"LITTLE CHRISTMAS EVE" is a Norwegian tradition that is almost as splendid as Christmas Eve itself. We hold it on December 23 and hold a special party for friends and relatives who will be with their own families on the real Christmas Eve. Often we also invite a family that has just moved into our neighborhood or a needy family. We celebrate with a lovely dinner, games, and prizes. This really helps us to get the Christmas spirit.

WE HAVE "MINI-CHRISTMASES" all through the month of December. Dad will declare a mini-Christmas and take the whole family skiing, or Mom will present a present to one member of the family who needs a lift. Anyone in the family who wants to do something nice for someone else can declare a mini-Christmas. It makes the whole month glow.

WE HAVE A CHRISTMAS FIRESIDE on the first Sunday of December. We invite about fifty people to a buffet dinner, after which we sing carols and some of the group sing solos.

FOR ABOUT TWELVE DAYS BEFORE CHRISTMAS when we were young, we'd put yellow glass plates, one for each of us, across the window ledge in the dining room every night. We'd sprinkle them with salt for Santa's reindeer. In the morning the salt would be gone, and in its place, if we'd been very good that day, we'd find a treat. If we'd been bad, a piece of coal would mar the sunshine yellow of the plate and increase our resolve to mend our ways. Santa's helpers never failed to judge our behavior and mete out the appropriate reward.

ON THE EVENING OF DECEMBER 6, two special visitors rap loudly on our door. Dad throws it open, and in stomps Sinter Claus and his helper, Black Pete. Sinter Claus asks each of us if we've been good all year. If the answer is no, he spanks his partner, Black Pete, amid much merriment and pleading for mercy. Then they fill our wooden shoes with treats and take off into the night, leaving us very excited about the Christmas season.

MUSIC PERMEATES OUR HOME at Christmastime, ranging from recordings of *Messiah* to simple Christmas carols. Sometimes we turn off all the lights, light a big Christmas candle set in a wreath of greens, and sing carols together. Usually a little pot of spices is simmering in a pot on the stove for a special treat.

WE FILL A RED FELT BAG with little rhythm instruments, triangles, bells, and cymbals. When our family sings carols, even the little ones help make music with these instruments.

On December 1 we make a list of twenty-five Christmas carols and sing one each night until Christmas.

EARLY IN DECEMBER we go on a shopping spree and then have our pictures taken with Santa. We display the pictures from year to year on a bulletin board in our family room. It's fun to see ourselves grow from age one to age sixteen on Santa's lap.

DURING THE THANKSGIVING HOLIDAY we make a big Christmas calendar of all the special events we want to attend or create. The children are always included in one adult function, such as attendance at a ballet, musical program, or drama. We have an annual sleigh-riding party with another family and afterwards eat soup by the fireplace and sing carols. We try to remember that Christmas is not just for children, but for grown-ups as well, and careful planning can help make it memorable for everyone.

OUR GRANDPARENTS always have a grandchildren's party, with no adults included except for grandparents. Grandmother has a special Christmas tree decorated with the children's pictures in little frames. She calls them her Christmas jewels.

ONE OF OUR SPECIAL TREASURES is a collection of Christmas stories and poems to which we add new ones each year. We put them in a giant red looseleaf binder and read and share throughout the Christmas season. We love to choose old favorites as well as new ones to read each night of the Christmas season.

GRANDMA MAKES NEW PAJAMAS for us every Christmas. The Sunday before Christmas we always have dinner at her house. Then everyone dons his or her new pair of pajamas, and we have a parade.

BEGINNING IN NOVEMBER, Dad's workshop sports a new sign, Santa's Workshop. There Dad paints and renews bikes and other toys, and no one can enter without permission. Sometimes, if we have a project of our own, we can arrange in advance with Dad to use Santa's Workshop too, and Dad might even become our helper.

WE DESIGN AND MAKE A PIÑATA with strips of newspaper smeared with homemade flour paste and wrapped in layers around a balloon. Everybody helps paste on the final fringed layers of colored tissue paper. During December the piñata hangs in the dining room, mysteriously filled with goodies and little prizes. On Christmas Eve each of us takes a turn at being blindfolded and then trying to break the piñata open with a broomstick. We all share the goodies inside.

WE SAVE CHRISTMAS CARDS from year to year and use them for placecards, to decorate packages, or to make a Christmas alphabet book. For the alphabet book, we print one letter of the alphabet on each page of a large scrapbook. Then we each search through the cards for pictures of things that begin with the letters we've been assigned. For example, A is for the angel, B is for Bethlehem, C is for cattle, and D is for the donkey Mary rode. When one alphabet book is complete (and sometimes it takes two Christmases to do it), we begin another one. We all want one of these scrapbooks to take with us when we leave home.

WE MAKE A PAPER CHAIN on Thanksgiving day, with alternating red and green links, one for each day until Christmas. We hang the chain on the refrigerator, and every night at bedtime we take off one link and burn it. Thus we can keep track of how many days are left until Christmas.

OUR CHRISTMAS CHAIN has links of various colors, with blue reserved for Sundays and gold for Christmas Eve. We remove one link every morning. Inside each link, Mother writes an activity to do the day that link is removed, such as read a Christmas story at dinner, bake cookies, or decorate the Christmas tree.

A variation of this tradition is an advent calendar. Each of the days before Christmas is marked on the calendar by a little ornament or a pocket for a special treat for the children. Some advent calendars are made of green felt in the shape of a Christmas tree, with the last day, Christmas Eve, marked by a star or angel atop the tree.

WE BORROWED FROM GERMAN TRADITION and light candles on an advent wreath each evening at dinnertime, starting on December 1. The small wreath of evergreens with four red candles on it centers the dining room table. We burn one candle the first week in December, two the second week, three the third week, and all of the candles on Christmas Eve.

ON DECEMBER 1, a beautifully wrapped present appears as a centerpiece on our dinner table. Inside is a prize to be awarded

for the best-decorated room. We spend many happy hours getting our rooms ready for Christmas—first cleaning, then decorating. (Sometimes we decorate just our doors.) On judging
night, the entire family visits each room and makes a decision
on who wins the prize.

LIGHTING LUMINARIES on Christmas Eve is a tradition at
many homes. To make the luminaries, use brown paper lunch
bags, all the same size. Turn one inch of each bag to the outside, to form a cuff. Pour sand or soil into the bag to a depth of
about two inches. Then place a candle in the center of the
sand. If a bag tips over, the sand will snuff out the candle, so it's
safe to use them to decorate outdoors (they shouldn't be used
indoors).

One family places about two hundred luminaries in the
snow on their lawn to spell out the words "Merry Christmas."
Another family uses them to outline their porch and front
path, to light the way of the Christ child. This custom origi-
nated in Mexico and is used extensively in the southwestern
United States. Have everyone in the family help light the candles, so they will burn evenly.

WE CREATE A MINIATURE SCENE from a clinker—a chunk
of rock from a coal furnace. We usually pick these up at a
church or school. We soak the clinker in a solution of 1 part liquid bluing, 2 parts salt, and 4 parts water. We pour the solution
over the clinker repeatedly for five or ten minutes. Within a
few hours it changes into a hunk of beautiful white crystals. We
complete the scene with miniature figures, animals, and trees.

AN ANTIQUE TRUNK serves as a chest in our living room. At Christmastime we open the trunk lid, revealing the red velvet lining, and fill the trunk to the brim with Christmas presents.

ON OUR CHRISTMAS TREE we hang a little Santa that has been with the family for three generations. Every ornament on our tree has a story. We add a new one every year. Dad picks it out with great care and presents it to the family on Christmas Eve.

MANY YEARS AGO I printed the story "Keeping Christmas," by Henry Van Dyke, on a lightweight, bright green posterboard cut in the shape of a Christmas tree. This poster is hung on the door of our dining room each year for all to read the story. Teenage and adult family members understand its message and think a little deeper about the true meaning of Christmas.

A MUST AT OUR HOUSE is a gift from each of us for Jesus. We earn the money for the gifts ourselves. Our gifts have included a new hymnbook presented to our ward, a book for the church library, and a toy for the nursery. Sometimes we give special items to a needy family.

WE GIVE A BOOK to each of our children every Christmas so that they can build their own libraries. The books are chosen carefully for their lasting value.

THE CHILDREN IN OUR FAMILY always fill the stockings for our parents. Each child writes a letter to each parent telling them how much they are loved and appreciated. These are slipped into their stockings and are often the most treasured of all their Christmas gifts.

UNDER OUR PILLOWS each Christmas morning is a traditional letter from Santa that emphasizes the good things we've done in the past year and encourages us to be even better. We keep our letters in our own special binders and find ourselves re-reading them when we need a lift.

WE DRAW FAMILY NAMES on Christmas Eve. We don't tell whose name we drew. We have until the next evening to think of a gift of love or service for that person. We write the planned gift down and put it in an envelope. The envelopes are opened on Christmas night. Often our gift is a promise to do something that person has wanted us to do for a long time. Last Christmas Father wrote a letter to one son promising to write his life story for him before the new year was over.

OUR GIFT TO JESUS is one of self-improvement. About the first of December we put up a large green felt tree, which we decorate with cutouts from beautiful old Christmas cards. While we are cutting them, we discuss traits we would like to improve in ourselves. Then on the back of each cutout, before we hang it on the tree, we write our pledge to improve in a particular trait through December. We all work hard to be true to our pledges so they will truly be a gift of self.

MOTHER MAKES RED NIGHTGOWNS and caps for the girls and red nightshirts and caps for the boys to wear every Christmas Eve. She also gives us new red sock booties each year. We all match, and we have a lot of laughter over it.

MANY YEARS AGO my sister gave me a ring in a tiny silver jewel box. In the box also was a note that said "return filled." I kept the box on my dresser for a year and returned it with a silver chain. Still in the bottom of the box was the penned note, "return filled." Over the years that tiny box has traveled back and forth many times. It challenges us to find a gift that fits both the box and the receiver.

SELECTING THE CHRISTMAS TREE is a treasured experience for our family, and we all help make the selection. We fill the air with Christmas carols as we drive from tree lot to tree lot till we find the one we want. Sometimes we visit a live Christmas tree farm and cut our own. Especially memorable are the times we have obtained the necessary permits to cut down our tree in the mountains. We fill the house with pine branches, draping them in swags, and fashion wreaths adorned with pine cones. Then we have a special tree-night supper by the fireplace, with hot chocolate and Christmas cookies for dessert.

OUR CHILDREN love to sleep in sleeping bags around the lighted Christmas tree the first night it is decorated. It extends the magic of the moment. Dad slips in later when they are all asleep and turns off the tree lights.

WE COVER OUR TREE with cookies to represent family members and what they are doing in their lives each year. These are elaborately decorated with frosting. For example, the year one son graduated from college, his cookie wore a mortar-board and tassel.

WE PLAY CHRISTMAS MUSIC and sing along as we decorate our tree. When the lights are in place, we are ready to add the special ornaments. Mom gives three of them to each person as we sit in a circle on the floor. One at a time, as we put our decorations on the tree, we tell three things we are grateful for. Then we are given three more ornaments. This continues till all the ornaments are on the tree and our hearts are overflowing with gratitude.

WE BUILT A LITTLE VILLAGE to put around the base of our tree. It has grown into a miniature town and now has a little train that runs around one side. We watch all year for things to add to the scene. We have made many of the houses and bridges. Children love to play with it.

WHEN WE TAKE DOWN OUR TREE, we cut off all the branches and use them as tinder for the fireplace. Then we cut the trunk of the tree into small diagonal chunks each about an inch or two thick. We write the year on each piece and then store the pieces in a bag. Each Christmas Eve as we sit by the fire, we throw into it a piece from each of the trees we have had before, in proper sequence. Seeing the date brings back memories of each year. Each of the children throw in the chip from his year of birth and for other special times. Now our married children are carrying on the tradition.

WE LIGHT A BIRTHDAY CANDLE at Christmastime to celebrate the birthday of Jesus. As we light the candle, Father reminds us all that we give presents to each other instead of to
Jesus because that is the way we do honor to Him.

MOTHER MAKES A HUGE BATCH of sugar cookie dough
and puts it in the refrigerator to cool. Then she takes a night
out while Dad goes creative with us children in the kitchen.
We roll and cut, bake and frost, and then decorate to our
hearts' content. Sometimes he gives little prizes for the best
cookies (most creative, most original, and most humorous).
We always clean up the mess before Mom comes home. The
cookies form part of the treat boxes we take to friends and
neighbors.

OUR CHRISTMAS BREAKFAST is always waffles topped
with vanilla ice cream, sliced strawberries or raspberries, and
whipped cream.

OUR FAMILY GATHERS BY THE FIRE on Christmas Eve to
sing carols. When we retire, we each carry a glowing candle to
our room, still softly singing the last verse of "Silent Night."

ON CHRISTMAS EVE we take candles and flowers to the
cemetery. We dig a hole in the snow and place a lighted candle

there. The snow protects the candle from the wind so it stays lighted. Then we stand a single flower in the snow by the candle. This is a custom from Finland that ties generations together.

ALL OF MOTHER'S FAMILY meet at our grandparents' home on Christmas Eve for a big dinner. In the center of the dining table is a house similar to a gingerbread house. Inside are small presents for everyone, and attached to each present is a ribbon that leads to a place card. When dinner is over, the dishes and food are cleared from the table. Then each of us pulls the ribbon attached to his place card to receive his gift. This is my great-grandmother's treat for Christmas Eve. Afterwards, we have a program with numbers from each family. Santa Claus drops in with oranges and candy canes, but we have to sit on his lap in order to get them. We draw names for Christmas, and we each get to open our gift from the person who has drawn our name. Then Grandpa tells the story of the first Christmas.

WE PLAY A CANDY-BAR GAME on Christmas Eve. At dinner everyone receives a candy bar with a number on it. Matching numbers are on some of the presents under the tree. Mom sets a clock periodically throughout the evening, and whenever it goes off, a number is called out. If it matches the number on our bar, we claim our present under the tree and open it. When all of the presents have been claimed, we enjoy eating the candy bars.

AFTER OUR CHRISTMAS EVE DINNER, we read the story of Christ's birth from Luke. Then we set up chairs for our gifts from Santa. Each of us is allowed to open one gift from under the tree. Then we hear Santa's bell (Dad ringing old sleigh bells that have been in the family for three generations), and everyone heads for bed. On Christmas morning we first open the presents from Santa that are on our chairs. Then, after breakfast, we open the gifts from under the tree.

WE DON'T HANG UP STOCKINGS in our family on Christmas Eve—we have a Christmas ball. Mother buys a number of small gifts, usually enough for five or six per person. Then we all sit in a circle on the floor surrounding the pile of gifts. Mother starts off by selecting a gift and wrapping it in the end of a two-inch-wide roll of crepe paper. The next person adds another gift to the growing roll, and we continue on around the circle until all the gifts have been wrapped into the ball. We sing Christmas carols and laugh a lot as we make our selections, always hoping that the gifts we select will be the ones we will receive. After time out for treats and to stretch our legs, we form a circle again, this time sitting beside a different person. Then we unwind the ball slowly, and as our turn comes, we each receive the presents we uncover. We can choose to keep a present, give it away, or trade it for something else. Part of the joy is to be able to give something we receive to someone who wants it very much.

WE COLLECT NATIVITY SCENES and arrange and display them in our home for Christmas. But the best nativity scene is the one we act out in a nearby barn. Wearing improvised costumes, we perform by lantern light each year on Christmas Eve. As we come back to our warm fireside, we are humbled and in the mood for Christmas.

CHRISTMAS EVE has gradually evolved into a very special time at our house. When we awake that morning, a feeling of magic is in the air. In the morning we wrap last-minute gifts and set the dinner table with our finest linen, china, and crystal goblets. The table seems to get bigger every year to accommodate our growing family and special guests.

By midmorning, the presents are piling up under the tree and guests are beginning to arrive for the festivities. Tantalizing aromas of favorite foods drift through the house, reminding everyone of the excitement to come.

At two o'clock we all sit down to a table spread with a magnificent Christmas feast: stuffed pork chops, vegetables, cranberries, fruit salad, green salad, homemade breads, frozen raspberry jam, and sparkling grape juice. Most of the food is prepared ahead, so there are few last-minute preparations. We talk and eat and enjoy one another's company until the six lighted candles in the center of the table are burning low. Then the pudding is served. Sometimes it is English trifle, sometimes Norwegian rice pudding. Buried deep within layers of whipped cream, fruit, and pudding are four or five almonds. Each lucky person who bites into an almond receives a special gift.

After the dishes are done, we go to the living room for the evening's activities. A favorite tradition started one year when Mother wanted to do something special for the men and older boys in the family. She bought a number of sale ties and wrapped them in Christmas paper. After dinner she emerged with a huge basket of these gaily wrapped presents.

Each male guest then drew a number from a hat. Number one could choose any of the presents he wanted. "Wow! A tie! Thanks, Mom!" Then the next person could take either a wrapped present or the first person's tie. "Great! A tie! Just what I needed!" This continued, with each person taking another's tie or opening a new present—and we soon realized all the gifts were ties. If a person's tie was taken, he could choose another one from the basket or from someone's neck. Soon the participants were bargaining ties right off each other's necks and trying to get rid of the ones they didn't like. When they had all had a turn, number one was feeling cheated—so Mom announced that they could go through the numbers again. This has evolved into a favorite tradition, and Mom always includes at least one really outrageous tie to add to the hilarity.

After the ties are all sorted out, the youngest children don flowing robes and, with a little help from the grown-ups, enact the nativity scene as one of the men reads selections from Luke.

Next, a gaily decorated piñata appears, dangling from the end of a long pole. Each child, from youngest to oldest, can have a turn at swinging a stick to try to burst the piñata open. The younger children may stand up and keep their eyes open, but the older ones must kneel, blindfolded. When the piñata is finally split, candy and small gifts fly out, and the children scramble to pick them up.

By this time many of the guests must leave for the long drive home. Those who remain bundle up warmly and visit neighboring homes, singing Christmas carols and delivering homemade treats.

Just before we go to bed, Dad stretches a wire across the mantel, and we hang up our stockings. At our home we don't use fancy felt stockings; rather, we use nylon stockings or knit stockings that will stretch.

During the night, after the children have gone to bed, Santa silently slips in and fills the stockings and arranges presents under the tree. Then he puts dozens of brightly colored balloons among the branches of the tree to be admired the next morning when presents are opened. (And how they survive the prickly needles, we never know.)

NEWLYWEDS OFTEN have to adjust as they meld two different sets of traditions into one life-style. The trick is to be able to take the best and most meaningful traditions from each partner and put them together with love and creativity for a distinctive new family.

One young couple, spending their first Christmas together, rose early on Christmas morning, and the bride started to rush eagerly toward the living room to see the tree. With a wounded look, her husband stopped her short and said, "Well, aren't we going to march first?"

"March? What do you mean march?"

"We always march," he announced firmly.

When someone says "We always . . ." in that emphatic way, you know you've bumped up against a family tradition. So the bridegroom proceeded to lead the family march, with the bride behind, her hands on his shoulders. They marched in and out of every room in the house, up and over beds, enthusiastically singing their favorite Christmas carols as they went. Finally he started singing "Silent Night" softly, and they entered the living room, where the Christmas tree glittered and stockings bulged with gifts.

Later, as three little girls were added to the family, each one joined in the marching, first in their daddy's arms, then tagging along behind. As years flew by, many childhood memories faded, but the marching tradition continued. When the eldest daughter became engaged and her fiancé was coming to spend Christmas with the family, she hesitantly asked her father, "Do we have to march this year?"

"Of course we have to march," he told her. "We always march!"

"But he won't understand, Dad. He'll think we're all crazy."

But march they did, and the fiancé was part of the fun, singing the carols as loudly as anyone. And now the three daughters all have families of their own, and everybody in the extended family marches on Christmas morning.

SANTA ALWAYS COMES on Christmas morning at seven o'clock sharp. Dad gets up at 6:45 A.M. to light the fire and turn on the tree lights, and all the children climb into bed with Mom. Promptly at seven we hear a loud knock at the front door. Then we hear Dad say heartily, "Well, hello, Santa! Merry Christmas! Come in, Santa!" Santa blows a loud horn and stomps through the house, with Dad following along, carrying on a running, one-sided conversation: "Yes, I've been good, Santa. I've really been good. Stay away from that bedroom, Santa. Don't hurt those kids." We all bury our heads deep in the covers as Santa stomps into the room, still tooting his horn. He pats each of us on the head under the covers, with Mom and Dad loudly protecting their children. Then he stomps out, but he always leaves his horn.

When we hear Dad's final "Merry Christmas" and the front door slam, we all come out from under the covers. "Is he gone? Can we come out and see?" And then we go to the living room, where Christmas is revealed in all its glory.

Sometimes when Grandpa visits, he is the one who ushers Santa in, while Dad plays the game with the children. One thing we have noticed: there is never a footprint in the snow on the front porch or sidewalk after one of Santa's visits.

THE CHILDREN IN ONE FAMILY enjoy waking their parents up on Christmas morning in ingenious, original ways. One year, for example, they improvised a rhythm band to greet their parents; another year, the parents woke up to a rat-tat on the window, with a Santa face peeking in. Last year the children attached a timer to the stereo, and the whole house woke up at six o'clock in the morning to the sound of carols. The only thing the parents can expect for certain is that they will be awakened early.

WE ALWAYS GET DRESSED and gather together for family prayer before we go into the room where the Christmas tree is. It's against the family rules even to peek before we're all ready. Then we line up, from the youngest to the oldest, and throw open the door for the breathtaking view of the sparkling tree.

SOME FAMILIES have breakfast before they open presents. Others prefer to have the excitement first. Christmas breakfasts traditionally vary from fruit tucked into the stockings and eaten by the fire to formal meals served in the dining room with candles ablaze on an advent wreath. One family's tradition is a progressive breakfast as they travel to various relatives' homes, with others joining them along the way.

AFTER WE OPEN OUR PRESENTS, we each select one to give to a needy family. Beforehand, our parents select the needy family and decorate a box to be filled with food. Each of us rewraps our "sacrifice" gift and places it in the box. We all bundle up and help deliver the gifts, sing carols, and wish the recipients a merry Christmas. We were somewhat reluctant at first, but now we look forward to the joy we experience as we share.

Food, Glorious Food

Some of my earliest recollections are of Mother making taffy. Dad pulled the hot, sticky syrup nimbly into gleaming white ropes of satin. "Use your fingertips!" he always instructed us. But it was so much easier to grasp the hot taffy in our fists where the skin was not quite so tender. My tired arms always lost the endurance test, and the result would be a still sticky, translucent rope of taffy that suffered from too much handling and too little pulling.

Dad had a magical way with food, turning plain white sugar into fluffy balls of nut-filled divinity, or common flour and lard into doughnut treats. When Dad dressed a pork and Mother rendered out the lard, it was he who mixed and fried the doughnuts and piled the golden rings high to share with cousins, uncles, and aunts. But Mother won our hearts each Christmas when she made her smooth fondant and dipped it in rich dark chocolate.

On our ranch, in a sparsely settled corner of Idaho, we made our own entertainment and learned to make do with what we had. Money was scarce and the store was eight miles away, so cooking was a challenge in creativity. Often, after starting a recipe from a cookbook, we would discover three or four missing ingredients, forcing us to improvise. Many exotic concoctions resulted.

The sound of wheels rolling out of the driveway, taking Mother and Dad away from the ranch, was a signal for us to pull out the pots and pans and become inventive in the kitchen. Sometimes at the first signal of their return we'd shove the telltale pots and pans beneath our beds and jump under the quilts with all our clothes on, pretending to be fast asleep. Later we'd slyly scrub the pots and pans in secret and return them to their proper places. Coincidentally, Mother's back would always be turned, but often I'd catch a playful smile at her lips.

OUR FAMILY'S STAINED-GLASS COOKIES are a tradition that has evolved from many familiar aspects of the Christmas season: stained-glass windows, gift giving, and, of course, food.

One year we made huge "Christmas sun" stained-glass cookies to hang in the front window, surrounded by evergreens and blinking lights and drawing many comments from passers-by. Delighted with the response to our creation, we began making dozens of smaller cookies, each a work of stained-glass art, and gave them to friends and relatives.

Later, while we were searching for a creative but more substantial gift, we thought of making cookie boxes out of the dough. Each box we created was so beautiful that we knew we couldn't fill it with anything but love. On Christmas day special friends would receive these boxes, each a fragile box, transparent as glass on top, and encircled by a beautiful satin ribbon. Inside, a folded note said, "This may look like an empty box, but it is not. It is full of love and appreciation for the person you are and the joy you bring into my life."

Now many variations of this tradition are part of the Bateman holiday tradition. The once-complicated process has become easy, and after years of practice, the work goes quickly. But all who receive the stained-glass treats marvel at their exquisite beauty.

Directions for making our stained-glass cookie creations follow.

Step 1: Stained-Glass Cookie Cutters

You can buy cookie cutters, but it's fun to make your own. Using disposable aluminum pie plates, cut strips 1" by 3". Stand each strip on its edge and, following the sketches in the illustration, mold one strip into a triangle and another into a heart shape. Allow no overlap. Secure with sticky tape. Other possible patterns include circles, cloverleaf, diamond, or crescent.

Step 2: Window Glass Candy

2 cups sugar
½ cup light corn syrup
½ cup water
Flavoring and coloring

Combine sugar, corn syrup, and water in a saucepan. Cook mixture without stirring until a candy thermometer reads approximately 300° F. Add flavoring and food coloring. If additional colors are desired, quickly pour hot candy into separate warm pans with a drop or two of food coloring in each. Pour the hot, colored candy mixture onto aluminum foil to cool. Crack cool candy with a knife handle until it is in pieces small enough to conveniently store in small bottles. Note: Window Glass Candy may be made several days ahead and stored in a tightly covered container.

Step 3: Stained Glass Cookie Dough

½ cup shortening
1 ½ cups sugar
2 eggs
1 teaspoon vanilla extract
4 cups sifted flour
1 ½ teaspoons double-acting baking powder
½ teaspoon salt
4 to 5 teaspoons milk

In a large bowl, cream shortening, sugar, eggs, and vanilla. Sift together flour, baking powder, and salt; add gradually to shortening mixture. Stir in enough milk to form a fairly dry dough. Divide dough into four pieces; with your hands, mold each piece into a ball. Put each ball in a tightly covered dish and refrigerate about an hour.

Stained-Glass Cookies

Remove a section of dough from the refrigerator and roll it ¼ inch thick on a sheet of foil the size of your cookie sheet. Using an empty can or other round object five to eight inches in diameter, cut as many cookies as will fit on the foil. Place them close together; the dough will not spread. Use homemade cutters or commercial cutters to cut out designs in the cookies. If care is used in handling the foil, much of the cookie can be cut out. The more "stained glass" each cookie contains, the prettier it will be. Fill in the spaces with colored Window Glass Candy. Heat oven to 350° F. Bake 10 to 15 minutes, or until cookie is firm and candy has melted. Remove from oven before candy bubbles up and loses its transparency.

Giant Sun Cookie

Take one of the four sections of dough from the refrigerator. On a sheet of foil, and using a lightly floured rolling pin, roll the dough into a circle ¼ inch thick. Using an overturned bowl or similar item as a guide, cut a four-inch circle from the center of the dough. (Be careful not to cut the foil.) Using the triangle cutter, cut out triangular pieces of dough, ends pointing out, about half an inch from the outer edge of the circle. Try to estimate spacing before you cut them all. In the spaces between each triangle, cut out heart shapes, with their points toward the center. (Or you may use a design of your own creation.)

Trim the outer edge of your giant cookie with a knife so it is even, and place the entire cookie and its sheet of foil on a cookie sheet. Decorate with silver decors at points of triangles and between hearts. Fill each cutout with the desired color of Window Glass Candy pieces. Work carefully and fill only the hole. Mix colors, if you wish. Amount of candy for each cutout is determined by how thick you want your "glass" to be.

Cut out eyes, a mouth, and a nose from the extra dough, and place them next to the cookie on the cookie sheet. Heat oven to 350° F. Bake for 10 to 15 minutes, or until cookie is firm and candy has melted. Remove from oven before candy bubbles up and loses its transparency. Immediately after removing the cookie from the oven, press the eye, nose, and mouth pieces lightly into the melted candy. If there are any holes in the "windows," quickly spread the hot candy with a toothpick before it cools.

Cookie Boxes

On aluminum foil, roll out dough ¼ inch thick, using the pattern given or one of your own design, and cut out cookie box pieces. Do not try to pick any of the pieces up; just remove the excess dough from around the edges.

With cookie cutters, make a design on the piece that will form the lid of the cookie box (the largest pattern piece). Fill cutouts with Window Glass Candy, and bake as directed above. Remove cookies from oven and cool.

When cookie box pieces are cool, assemble the box. Make a colorless batch of Window Glass Candy in a wide, flat pan. When candy reaches the hard-crack stage (300° F.), carefully dip the edge of each piece in it. Stick pieces together, starting with the bottom of the box and adding side pieces one at a time. The candy hardens quickly, so aim carefully as you assemble the pieces. It doesn't matter if some corners are crooked or the lid doesn't fit exactly right. You'll improve with practice. To make the lid stay on better, dip all four edges of the lid piece in the candy. (Be careful with the hot melted candy. Keep small children at a safe distance, and have someone help by holding the pieces as you work.)

If you prefer, you may use royal icing to hold the pieces of the box together. Allow the icing on each piece of the cookie box to dry completely before the next piece is added.

Stained-glass cookies may be used as Christmas tree ornaments, house decorations, "phantom family" treats, or special surprises for friends and relatives. Practice makes perfect; don't become discouraged if you have difficulties in making them at first. I have experienced many a burned, broken, misshapen, backwards, or crumbly cookie.

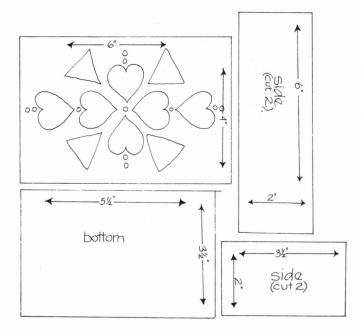

WE'VE BECOME PROFICIENT in making decorated cakes for special occasions. With lots of work, imagination, and practice, our cakes, including wedding cakes, have become masterpieces of artistry in sugar.

One of the most intriguing traditions associated with our decorated cakes is the sugared flowers that adorn their layers. Sugar, gracefully beading on the fragile petals of gladiolus, roses, or violets, captures in crystal beauty the flowers' form and color. Yet the sugared flowers are simple enough for even the most inexperienced decorator to make.

Select only flowers that are at the peak of freshness. Pick them when petals are crisp, or place them in water in a cool place until petals become crisp. Fasten a cake rack to the top of a bottle or can with masking tape to make a rack where the flowers can hang to dry. To dry the flowers, tuck the end of the stem in the rack and let the flower hang down.

Combine 2 egg whites and ½ cup of water, beating just enough to break up the egg white and keep the foaming to a minimum. Pour the clear liquid into a small bowl, keeping all foam out. Rinse flower in cool water (to get rid of any bugs), then dip into mixture of egg white and water. Turn flower face down on a plate to drain off moisture. Shake off the excess liquid by rolling the stem between your fingers, whirling the flower. The surface of the petal should be damp but not dripping.

Holding the flower over a sheet of waxed paper, sprinkle all surfaces with sugar. Dry the flower upside down on the rack by sticking a toothpick through the stem; lay the toothpick crosswise on the rack, with the flower hanging down. Allow to dry for an hour, or until petals are crisp and flower holds its shape.

Flowers that do well include the following:

Gladiolus. Cut off individual flowers except for the tip blossoms. Rearrange when dry.

Roses. These work well if they are quite open and very fresh. Heavy buds or closed flowers don't dry well; they just ooze wet sugar.

Violets. These are dainty as well as delicious.

Chrysanthemums. Spider mums are especially nice.

Daisies. These hold their shape and color very well.

Lilacs. These stay beautiful for a long time. Single blossoms can be clipped off and used for dainty effects.

Apple blossoms. These may be done in clusters or singly.

Baby's breath. This keeps perfectly without sugaring and can be used to fill in around your sugared arrangements.

As a general rule, flowers that hold up well may be sugared successfully. When choosing flowers other than those listed above, be sure to check with your florist. Some species are poisonous and should not be eaten.

"NECESSITY IS THE MOTHER OF INVENTION." On a triple date, three coeds proved this adage. "Don't worry," their dates had said, "just dress casually. This will be a creative date." When all three couples were in the car, the girls looked at one another apprehensively. "Here you go, girls," the driver said, giving his date a ten-dollar bill. "You are buying dinner for the evening. We'll plan the entertainment." With that, the gallant young men left their dates in the grocery store parking lot, promising to return in thirty minutes.

At first the girls were confused, but soon a family tradition came to the rescue. Cindy told her bewildered friends about a "magic recipe" her mother had that was quick and easy to prepare, but pleased even the most sophisticated guests. The girls quickly made up a shopping list, and when their dates returned for them thirty minutes later, they had purchased the ingredients for their ten-dollar dinner. Within forty-five minutes the meal was on the table, and the young men gazed in admiration. Here is the recipe, which serves four to six:

Mexican Pile-up

1 pound ground beef
Salt
Pepper
15- or 20-ounce can refried beans
Tomato sauce or water
1 large package corn chips
½ pound Cheddar cheese, shredded
½ head lettuce, shredded
1 onion, finely diced
2 large tomatoes, finely cubed
1 pint sour cream
1 small can chopped olives
Hot sauce (optional)

Brown ground beef in frying pan until crumbly. Season with salt and pepper. Dilute refried beans with small amount of tomato sauce or water; heat. Arrange each ingredient attractively in a serving bowl. Set bowls on table in this order: corn chips, hot ground beef, hot refried beans, shredded cheese, shredded lettuce, diced onion, cubed tomato, sour cream, chopped olives, and hot sauce, if desired. Beginning with the corn chips, each person piles ingredients on top of one another on his plate. Caution: Start with small amounts, or the food will really pile up. Count on serving seconds.

NEIGHBORS FOR MILES AROUND knew about Mother's famous homemade ice cream. Each time we made the exquisite treat, it was a major family project. The magic began when we pulled great hunks of ice from the damp sawdust of the icehouse, a miraculous unveiling in hot July, and crushed it for the ice cream freezer. Thick cream, skimmed from the top of a milk can, was added to sugar and fruits, and all were blended together into a mixture too delicious to resist.

Our arms ached as we turned and turned the squeaky crank of the freezer. Every time we paused to rest, fingers dipped into the bucket to test the half-frozen mixture. The reward was sweeter to the taste because a part of us had been sacrificed in its creation. Finally, after what seemed like years of waiting, we'd carefully pull the dasher from the ice cream and lick it clean, savoring every drop of sticky, fruity sweetness. The fun of making ice cream together never loses its traditional family charm.

Three-of-a-Kind Ice Cream

3 bananas
3 oranges
3 lemons
3 cups milk
3 cups whipping cream
1 ½ cups sugar (may use honey)

Crush the bananas, juice the oranges and lemons, and mix bananas and juices together. Add milk, cream, and sugar. Freeze according to ice cream maker directions.

THE AROMA OF SPICY GINGERBREAD COOKIES fills our home sometime around the first of December, and soon everyone gets in on the act of building a gingerbread house. Nothing tastes better than warm gingerbread, and even Dad, drawn to the kitchen like a bee to a blossom, gets his share of the scraps.

Problems in making gingerbread houses usually fall into two areas: (1) making the pieces fit together properly, and (2) sticking the walls together. Here are some suggestions to help you avoid such problems and have a very satisfying experience the first time you try to make a gingerbread house. (If you are a beginner, it may be better to do the first two steps over two days rather than one.)

Step 1: Obtain a good pattern or create your own. Using the pieces of your pattern, make the house first in thin cardboard, and stick it together with masking tape, making sure all the pieces fit together well. Then take it apart and use the cardboard pieces as your pattern. Save the cardboard in an envelope and use it again each year. I write out my recipe for the entire house on one of the large roof pieces; then it is always available when I get the pattern out. If two roof or wall pieces are identical in size, use separate pieces of cardboard for each so there will be no confusion when you lay out the pattern to cut the gingerbread.

Use the largest cookie sheet you have that will fit in your oven, and lay out the pattern pieces so they just touch. Use the space to your best advantage, because the gingerbread between pattern pieces must also be cooked. Use additional sheets, if necessary, to lay out all the pieces. Then divide the dough according to the number of cookie sheets to be used, and roll it out to about ⅛-inch thickness on the greased sheets. To keep the dough from sticking to the rolling pin, pull a clean nylon stocking over it tightly and secure with rubber bands over the handles. Flour lightly. (When you are through, wash it under the tap and pat it dry with a towel.) You may wish to sprinkle the dough with granulated sugar; pressed in with a rolling pin, it gives a pretty, sugary texture to the finished gingerbread. It does, however, make the decorations a little more difficult to stick on.

Fit the pattern pieces on the rolled-out dough and cut around them with a sharp knife. Do not remove any of the dough shapes to avoid spreading or shifting of the design and misshaped pieces. Bake the entire marked sheet of dough at 350° F. for about 10 minutes; remove from oven when dough is set but still soft. Immediately cut around all the house pieces again with a paring knife. (It may help to lay the pattern pieces back on the cookie and cut around them, but this is not necessary; the shapes will remain true to the pattern.) Carefully lift out all the excess pieces and return cookie sheet with the houses pieces to the oven for another 5 minutes to firm up. Remove pan from oven and gently slide a spatula under each house piece to loosen from pan. Cool completely on pan; then place each piece carefully on a rack to complete the firming-up process.

Excess pieces can be cut into furniture pieces while still warm. This is a part of the project children enjoy participating in. Little candies, brightly colored and in various shapes, may be used as legs for chairs and tables. These should be added after the cookie shapes are completely cooled and hardened.

Step 2: Assemble all the materials needed to put the gingerbread house together and a base on which to assemble it. Our favorite base is a large, round mirror; a tray or piece of cardboard covered with foil may also be used. Some people use royal icing to hold the pieces together, but the easiest and fastest way is simply to melt sugar. Use a frying pan large enough so that the longest pattern *edge* you wish to glue will fit flat in the pan. An electric frying pan is especially good for this.

To melt the sugar, put one cup of granulated sugar in the frying pan and turn to high heat. Stir with a fork until the sugar melts and becomes a light golden brown liquid. Turn the heat down to 300° F., and quickly put the pieces of the gingerbread house together. Dip into the shallow syrup both edges of the two pieces you want to connect, then connect them. Continue adding walls, then the roof.

For the roof, dip the two edges that form the ridgepole. Connect them, then lay the roof on the gable, holding it for a minute until the candy hardens. You can seal the edges around the eaves later with royal icing. In five minutes or less you can put the whole house together so sturdily that it will stand much

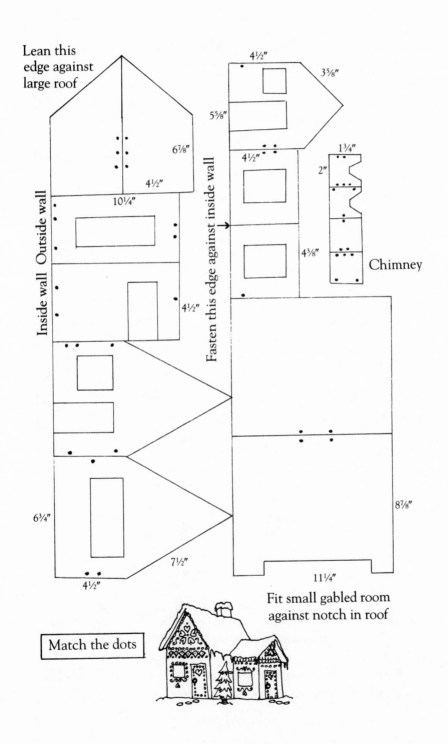

Lean this
edge against
large roof

Inside wall Outside wall

6⅞"

4½"

10¼"

4½"

6¾"

4½"

7½"

Fasten this edge against inside wall

4½"

3⅝"

5⅝"

4½"

4⅜"

1¾"

2"

Chimney

8⅞"

11¼"

Fit small gabled room
against notch in roof

Match the dots

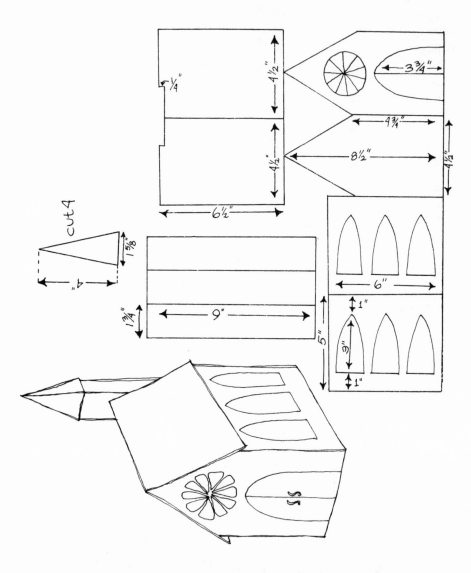

handling. (Do not do this step when small children are around. Melted sugar can cause painful burns if not treated with great caution.)

Part of the charm of the house is the yard or garden. We like a duck pond, a curved pathway, a tall tree, and lots of other interesting side scenes. For the tree, use any shrub that branches well and looks like a miniature tree. To form the tree base, force the trunk in the hole of a thread spool cut in half crosswise; then attach the base to the mirror with double-stick tape (sticky both sides), florist tape, or royal icing.

Now comes the fun. Fill several pastry tubes with different colors of royal icing. Set bowls of colored candies nearby, and begin decorating. If neighbor children drop in, let them help too. Every wall and gable, as well as the windows and doors, can be decorated differently; but when everyone is finished, the house will have great charm and beauty.

Here are some ideas for decorating:

1. Create a path to the house with flat candies, such as Neccos or mints.

2. Cover the tree branches with Snow Icing (see recipe below) and add bright candy decorations, if desired. Swirl snow around the base of the tree to cover the spool.

3. After the outside of the house has been decorated, swirl Snow Icing on the roof and pull it down to form icicles around the eaves. This will help cover any faults in the architecture, such as at wall corners and where the chimney is attached to the roof. Perch a miniature Santa and reindeer atop the snowy roof.

4. Lay a thick "shag rug" on the floor inside the house, using tinted coconut. Put the furniture in through the open doors and windows.

5. Add a light inside the house to give it a warm glow. Just before you put the roof on, hang a bent paper clip in the melted sugar along the ridgepole of the roof, and loop over it a little light, such as a night light. Or shine a small high-intensity light through a back window of the house.

6. Create a fence by standing chocolate-covered orange sticks about an inch apart around the edge of the mirror or base; connect them with strings of piped royal icing, and cap each one with a tuft of icing snow.

When people ask if we keep our gingerbread house from year to year, we emphatically answer no. That would defeat the purpose. It is the building and creating of the house together as a family that is special.

Sometime after New Year's Day, our children invite all their friends to join them for a "smash party." After removing any treasured figures from the gingerbread house, we count to three and then the children demolish the house. The children bargain for favorite pieces, and they carry them away in plastic bags. Next year we'll build an even better house!

Snow Icing

4 egg whites
2 cups granulated sugar
½ cup water
½ teaspoon cream of tartar

In a clean glass bowl (don't use plastic), beat egg whites at high speed. Continue beating while you prepare the syrup. In a heavy saucepan, combine sugar, water, and cream of tartar; bring to boil with lid on so steam will melt crystals on sides of pan. Remove lid and continue boiling to soft-ball stage (240° F.). Pour hot syrup in a fine stream into egg whites, beating as you pour; beat for about five more minutes. Spread the icing quickly on the roof and grounds of the gingerbread house, pulling it down into icicles around the eaves (don't try to go back and make icicles afterwards).

MODELING WITH CLAY AND DOUGH and doing finger painting delight children, who enjoy the texture and feel of these materials. At our house it's traditional to model with frosting. At Christmas we make small figures to put in and around our gingerbread house, using this recipe:

Modeling Frosting

1½ cups powdered sugar
1 egg white
¼ teaspoon cream of tartar

Beat all ingredients together until mixture forms stiff peaks that will follow the spoon up when it is raised and will hold their shape. Put an additional half cup powdered sugar on a plate, and add half the frosting; work sugar and frosting with your fingers as you would work flour into bread dough, until it forms a smooth elastic ball and does not stick to the fingers. If dough is sticky, roll it in a little more powdered sugar and knead again. If dough is crumbly, work in a little more frosting. Keep dough and frosting each tightly covered with plastic wrap at all times; they dry very quickly.

Pinch off a small amount of dough at a time as you model your figures. To stick parts together, touch the edges to a dampened napkin, or dampen your fingers and touch the frosting. A wing can then be attached to a bird, or a hat to a snowman. When an object is finished, dry it on wax paper for about 24 hours.

Frosting figures can be painted with cake coloring and an eyeliner brush or fine watercolor brush. They are fragile to handle, but they add a great deal of charm to your gingerbread house.

Modeling frosting can also be used to make a beautiful rose to grace the center of a cake. For a two-tone rose, use a small ball of white and a small ball of pink frosting. Flatten them together between the thumb and finger to form a petal; press it thin along the upper edge and curl slightly outward. Curve the bottom edge to form a cone. Add another petal, overlapping and pinching off the excess at the bottom; continue adding petals until the rose is the desired size. Cover your cake with white frosting; then press tinted coconut lightly around the sides. To tint coconut, put a few drops of water in a bowl. Add a drop of the desired cake color and the coconut; work the color through the coconut with your fingers until it is even. Or put a few drops of water, a few drops of cake coloring, and the coconut in a small jar; cover, and shake until coconut is desired color.

Modeling Frosting may be used to make many other types of decorations for birthday cakes. We have made turtles, frogs, basketballs, baseballs, guitars, and trombones. Let your imagination work for you. The figures and decorations can be colored two ways:

1. Tint the frosting before modeling. Divide it into small bowls and add the desired colors. Then model your figures.

2. Model figures in white frosting. Allow creations to dry overnight. Then, using watercolor brushes and cake coloring, (paste-type is best), color in all the details of the figures: eyes, mouth, nose, hair, buttons, vests, ruffles, and so forth. When the color dries, the figures are ready to adorn your cake or to set in and around your gingerbread house.

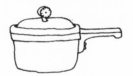

ON OUR FAMILY TRIP TO EUROPE, we found high prices, though our budget was low. But we set out for five months of traveling and camping in our Volkswagen campmobile. Since butane gas for our camp stove was expensive and sometimes difficult to find, we discovered that cooking in a pressure cooker was a good way to conserve energy. We learned quickly how to shop wisely and where to buy basic foods. That is how our "Europe meal" was created. We put vegetables that take the longest to cook, such as carrots and onions, on the bottom of the pressure cooker; then we stacked potatoes, zucchini, and other faster-cooking vegetables on top. With only a few minutes of flame, pressure mounted within the pot and everything cooked at once. Nearly every night we ate steaming buttered vegetables with melted cheese and fresh bread. Since it was difficult to store meat in the camper, meat became a special treat rather than a regular part of the menu.

For weeks after our return home, though we were surrounded by shelves and shelves of supermarket specials, a welcome sight was our "Europe meal" eaten with cheese we brought home from Holland.

BREAD MAKING IN A FAMILY is a wonderful tradition. Aside from filling the house with tantalizing aromas, bread is also symbolic of the staff of life. When baking bread, Mother always let us mold our own little pans of biscuits. We loved to eat them with jam, even though they were hard little balls that did not even remotely resemble her beautiful golden loaves. They were ours, and we were proud.

NO ONE IS TOO OLD for the fun in our family when Mother makes special treats for holidays. Heart-shaped pink pancakes dripping with whipped cream and strawberries say "I love you" on Valentine's Day morning. For Halloween, bright orange pancakes with chocolate chip eyes stare ominously up from a pool of black molasses. Hot cereal is colored green on St. Patrick's Day, and the green fruit juice tastes strangely familiar. In fact, on St. Patrick's Day even the butter is green, and so are the mashed potatoes and milk.

MOM GIVES A COOKIE PARTY around the first part of December. Friends and relatives are invited, and each one brings a big batch of her favorite cookies and a stack of recipe cards. Some of each kind are enticingly displayed on a big table and

sampled by all. The remainder are then divided up, and everyone takes home about fifteen or twenty different kinds of
cookies to freeze. The new recipes are filed away for easy refer-
ence.

AN ICE CREAM MOUNTAIN is our family tradition, usually
at Christmas but sometimes at other special events as well. We
line a big bowl with graham cracker crust and then add layers of
chocolate and vanilla ice cream. We freeze the "mountain"
solid, then unmold it and decorate with goodies, such as cher-
ries, nuts, and whipped cream.

Index

Activities: for New Year's Eve,
100-101; for New Year's Day,
101-2; for Easter, 104-6; on
Christmas Eve, 128-31. *See also*
Birthdays
Advent calendar and wreath, 121
Affection, showing, 55-56
Afternoons, traditions involving,
18-19, 27
Alphabet book, 120
Antiques, collecting and refinishing,
65
Appendages, Society of, 84
Apple pie, 6-7
Appreciation of world, 56-57
Aprons, traditions with, 8, 86, 102
Arm-chair travelers, 79-80
Artwork, displaying and keeping, 48
Attitude, positive, 48-50

Back rubs, 16
Backwards tie and apron, 8
"Bad kid" routine, 92-93
Balance scale to weigh babies, 86
Ball, Christmas, 129
Bands, family, 70-72
Bank account for children, 34-35

Basket, Easter, 105
Bathroom, chatting sessions in, 15-16
Baths to entertain children, 50-51
Be-kind-to-Mary week, 47
Bike riding as family, 79
Binder, looseleaf, for babies, 87
Biography on birthday, 98
Birth traditions, 83, 86-90
Birthday Book, 91-92
Birthday(s): like home, 3; cards, 64,
94; diaries read on, 88; Dr. Seuss
party, 91-92; "bad kid" routine,
92-93; night out with Dad, 93;
file folder, 93; wake-up, 93-94;
decoration of birthday room, 94;
matching clothes, 94; in
December, 94-95; choosing cake,
95; toothpicks in cake, 95; pie, 95;
candle, 95-96, 127; meals, 96; hot
cereal, 96; gifts to mother, 96-97;
Saint Bernard dogs, 97; party at
sixteen, 97; gold necklace, 97;
name on cane, 97; biography, 98;
letter to oneself, 98; father's
interview on, 98; house, 98-99;
month, 99
Black Pete, 118

Blow by the Blanket, 52
Book, family trip, 76
Books: on trips, 77; for Christmas, 123
Bottle with daisy, 8-10
Bottles, playing, 71
Box for traveling, 75
Bread making, 153
Breakfast, Christmas, 127, 134
Buddy system, 78
Budget books, teenagers' use of, 37-39
Budgets, children's participation in, 34
Business, family, 42

Cabin, trip to, 48-50
Cakes, traditions with, 93-95, 99-100
Calendar, Christmas, 119, 121
Camping out overnight, 78
Candle, birthday, 95-96, 127
Candles and flowers in cemetery, 127-28
Candy on Valentine's Day, 102
Candy-bar game, 128
Cane, name on, 97
Cards, traditions with, 64, 94, 116, 120
Caroling: with harp, 72; on Halloween, 108; with wish cards, 116; each day till Christmas, 118-19; by fire, 127; during Christmas march, 132
Catering business, 42
Celebrations on Fourth of July, 106-7
Cemetery, candles and flowers in, 127-28
Cereal, hot, 96
Chains, Christmas, 121
Chairs, traditions with, 52-53
Chandelier, crystal, 23-24
Chicago, trips to, with mother, 46-47
Children, helping, to develop, 58-59
Chores, price tags on, 39
Christening clothes, 87
Christmas: pre-Christian influences, 114; quality, 115; nativity scenes, 115-16, 129, 131; needy families, 116, 134; wish cards, 116; caroling, 116, 118-19, 127; gift-of-love tree, 116-17; "little Christmas Eve," 117; mini-Christmases, 117; fireside, 117; twelve days before, 118; Sinter Claus and Black Pete, 118; music, 118-19; Santa's lap, 119; calendar, 119; grandchildren's party, 119; stories and poems, 119; pajamas, 120; Santa's workshop, 120; piñata, 120, 131; alphabet book, 120; paper chains, 121; advent calendar, 121; advent wreath, 121; room decorating, 121-22; luminaries, 122; scene from clinker, 122; antique trunk, 123; ornaments on tree, 123; poster with story, 123; gift for Jesus, 123-24; books for children, 123; parents' stockings, 124; letter from Santa, 124; drawing family names, 124; gift of self-improvement, 124; using red for, 125; "return filled," 125; selecting tree, 125; sleeping bags around tree, 125; cookies on tree, 126; decorating tree, 126; building village, 126; dates on pieces of tree, 126; birthday candle, 127; making cookies, 127; breakfasts, 127, 134; candles and flowers, 127-28; Eve dinner and gingerbread house, 128; candy-bar game, 128; Eve, gifts on, 129; ball, 129; Eve, dinner and tie- giving on, 130-31; morning march, 132; morning, Santa visits on, 133; waking up parents, 133; tree, viewing, 134; giving away presents, 134
Christmas tree: taking down, 101-2; decorated with pictures, 119; ornaments on, 123; selecting, 125; sleeping bags around, 125; cookies on, 126; decorating, 126; dates on pieces of, 126; presents under, 130; viewing, 134
Clean-ups, 59, 107-8, 111
Clinker, scene made from, 122
Coins as gifts, 87

Collage as gift, 87
Colors for special occasions, 85, 107, 121, 125
Communication between family members, 5-6
Conversation on deeper level, 15
Cookie boxes, 139-40
Cookies, stained glass, 136-40
Cookies, traditions with, 103, 126-27, 136-40, 153-54
Cooking, 135-36. *See also* Recipes
Corporation, family formed into, 30-31
Costumes, Halloween, 108
Customs, studying different, 57

Daisy, bottle with, 8-10
Dancing with mother, 16
Date, girls fixed dinner on, 142-43
Dates on pieces of Christmas trees, 126
Debt, staying out of, 33
December activities, 94-95, 117-18. *See also* Christmas
Decorations, traditions involving, 94, 103, 121-22, 126
Deer hunting season, 112-13
Diaries for babies, 88
Dictionary, Mama's, 55
Dinner: discussions at, 21-22, 32; on Easter, 104; on Thanksgiving, 110; on Christmas Eve, 128, 130
Discord, taping family, 67-68
"Do You Love Me?" 8
Do-it-yourself projects, 41
Dr. Seuss party, 91-92
Duplexes, children investing in, 29-30

Easter Monday, 110
Easter traditions, 104-6
Eggs, Easter, 104-5
Entertaining at parties, 61
Envy, coping with, 32
Errands, sharing, 18
Europe meal, 152

Families, visiting, on Halloween, 109
Family: strengthening life of, 2-4; communication between members in, 5-6; fund for, 31-32; finance report night for, 34; garden maintained by, 40, 60, 111-12; to provide for growth, 45; pictures of, 53-54; tapes of, 54; games played by, 56; honoring absent members of, 57; taping discord in, 67-68; bands formed from, 70-72; welcoming new members into, 84-85; goals of, on New Year's Eve, 101; gifts for needy, 116
Family business, 42
Family corporation, 30-31
Family histories, 57, 101
Family home evening, 84-85
Family reunions and get-togethers, 33, 58
Family Store, 37
Family traditions. *See* Traditions, family
Family trip book, 76
Family T-shirt Club, 84
File folder, 93
Finance report nights, 34
Fireside, Christmas, 117
Flag-raising ceremonies, 106-7
Flowers: sugared, 141-42; traditions with, 8-10, 77, 127-28, 141-42
Food, joy of making, 135-36
Food budget, saving on, 41
Foods for New Year, 99-100
Fourth of July traditions, 106-7
Frosting, 149-52
Fun nights without money, 32-33
Fund, maintaining family, 31-32

Games, playing, as a family, 56, 75
Garage sales, 41
Gardens, family, 40, 60, 111-12
Giant sun cookie, 139
Gift-of-love tree, 116-17
Gifts: anonymously making and giving, 24-25; from grandmother, 56, 85-86; to mother, 96-97; to extended families, 99; on Valentine's Day, 103; for needy families, 116, 134; on December 1,

121-22; for Jesus, 123-24;
Christmas, to family members,
124-25; "return filled," 125; on
Christmas Eve, 129-30
Gingerbread houses, 128, 144-50
Goals, setting, 18, 40, 101
Grandchildren's party, 119
Grandma Bag, 56
Growth, family to provide for, 45
Guesses of baby's weight, 87
Guests helping at party, 61

Halloween traditions, 108-9, 153
Harp used in caroling, 72
Hasler, Dr. Arthur, 1
Haunted house, 108
"Headlight start" on travels, 74
Hike, spring, 111
History, family, 57, 101
Home, building own, 43
Home movies, 53-54
Homing of salmon, 1-2
Honoring absent family members, 57
Hope chest, 85-86
Household management before
marriage, 43-44
Houses, traditions with, 43, 63-64,
98-99, 108
"How much do you love me?" 11
Hunts, Easter egg, 104-5
Hymns, using, 68

Ice cream, 89-90, 143-44, 154
Instructions left for children, 62-63
Interview with father, 17-18, 98
Ironing, surprise during, 15
Irritations, solving, 21

Jackson, Wyoming, 112
James, oldest son named, 89
Jelly beans, hunting, 105
Jenny Lake, 112
Jigsaw-puzzle message, 17
Jobs, obtaining, 37, 40

"Keeping Christmas," 123
"Kidnapping" of children in family, 52
King or Queen for a Day, 75

Labor Day traditions, 107-8
Lawn maintenance by children, 41-42
Lemonade, slogan of, 63-64
Letters: to husband, 10; round-robin,
20; put in suitcase, 74; from
hospital, 88; and diaries to babies,
88; to oneself, 98; on
Thanksgiving, 109; for Christmas,
124
"Like home" birthday, 3
Lincoln's birthday, 103
List of good qualities, 48
Love messages, 10-11
Luminaries for Christmas, 122

Mad chair, 52
Magic carpet, 79-80
Mailboxes, treats in, 26-27
Mama's Dictionary, 55
Management of household before
marriage, 43-44
Manger, straw to fill, 115
March, Christmas morning, 132
Matching clothes, 94
Meals, special, 96, 142-43, 152. See
also Breakfast; Dinner
Memory wall, 54-55
Messages, love, 10-11
Mexican pile-up, 142-43
Mini-Christmases, 117
Minitrips, ideas for, 80-81
Mirrors, messages on, 11
Modeling, 150-52
Money, raising or increasing, 29-30,
33, 40-42
Money management, 28-29
Music: effects of, 66-67; introducing,
in home, 67; child teaches, to
family, 68-69; playing, together as
family, 70-71; giving, 71-72; at
Christmastime, 118-19
Mysteries, devising, 23-25

Names, traditions with, 64-65, 69,
89-90, 124
Nativity scenes, 115-16, 129, 131
Necklace, gold, 97
New Year's traditions, 48, 99-102

Newspaper, front page of, 87
Night out with Dad, 93
Nights Up, 19-20
Noise making, 100
"No-money" fun night, 32-33
Notes with clues, 105
Nutcracker ballet, 101

Ornaments on Christmas tree, 123
Outfitting of children for school, 79
Overnighters, 78

Painting of tree, 55
Pajamas for Christmas, 120
Paper chains, 121
Parable of talents, 42
Parades on Fourth of July, 106-7
Parties, traditions involving, 59, 61,
    97, 106-7, 119
Pennies, hidden, on island, 112
People night, 57
Pets, naming, 64-65
Phantom Family, 26-27
Photographs of rocking chair, 53
Piano lessons, 68
Pictures, traditions involving, 12, 53,
    86, 101
Pies, traditions with, 6-7, 95
Piñata, 120, 131
Pixie autographs, 25-26
Plan, monthly, for spending, 35-36
Planning trips, 74, 81-82
Pockets for traveling, 76
Poems and stories for Christmas, 119
Potatoes, picking, 60
Presents. *See* Gifts
Presidents' birthdays, traditions on,
    103-4
Price tags on chores, 39
Problem solving, 51-52, 61-62
Pumpkin caroling, 108
Punishment by exclusion from chores,
    58-59

Quilts, making, 60, 85-86

Reading on trips, 77
Real estate for children, 29-30

Recipes: stained-glass cookies,
    136-40; window glass candy,
    137-38; giant sun cookie, 139;
    cookie boxes, 139-40; sugared
    flowers, 141-42; Mexican pile-up,
    142-43; three-of-a-kind ice cream,
    143-44; gingerbread houses,
    144-50; melted sugar, 146; snow
    icing, 149-50; modeling frosting,
    151-52; Europe meal, 152; ice
    cream mountain, 154
Recording of family discord, 67-68
Repairs, learning to make, 41
Resolutions, New Year's, 101-2
Restitution, helping family members
    make, 31
"Return filled" note, gifts with, 125
Reunions, family, 33, 58
Reward system, reverse, 76
Ring, gold, 25
Rituals and traditions, 2-4
Rocking chair used for photographs,
    53
Roots, establishing, 1-4
"Round-robin" letters, 20

Sacrificing for family members in
    trouble, 31
Saint Bernard dogs, 97
Saint Patrick's Day, 153
Sales, garage, 41
Salmon, homing of, 1-2
Santa Claus, 118-20, 133
Saving for purpose, 40
Scale, candy, to weigh babies, 86
School, preparing for start of, 112
Season traditions, 110-13
Seat cover with pockets, 77
Secondhand stores, use of, 35
Self-esteem, building, 46-47
Self-improvement, gift of, 124
Sensitivity meter, 7
Sewing, 46, 59-60
Shopping, traditions involving, 35,
    41, 111-12
Signal, secret identifying, 14
"Silent Night," 70-71, 127, 133
Sinter Claus, 118

Sleeping bags around Christmas tree, 125
Slides shown on New Year's Eve, 101
Snow icing, 149-50
Society of the Appendages, 84
Softball game on flooded lawn, 106-7
Solve-it-yourself room, 51-52
Solving of problems as game, 61-62
Song leader for family, 69
Songs, 69, 75-76. *See also* Caroling; Music
Spending plan, monthly, 35-36
Spook alley, 108
Spring traditions, 106, 110-11
Stained-glass cookies, 136-40
Stamps as gifts, 87
"Steak and rake" parties, 59
Stockings, Christmas, 124, 131
Stocks, gifts of, 30
Store, family, 37
Stores, secondhand, 35
Stories, use of, 77, 119
Straws to fill manger, 115
Styles, changing, reflected in pictures, 53
Sugar, melted, 146, 148
Sugared flowers, 141-42
Surprise afternoons off, 27
Swinging of sister in arms, 11

Tables Eve, 111
Taffy making, 135
Talents, salable, 40
Tape recorder, use of, 20-21
Tapes, traditions with, 54, 62-63, 67-68
Tartan and brooch for christening, 87
Teaspoon of water, 14-15
Teenagers managing own budgets, 37-39
Thanksgiving traditions, 60, 109-10
Thursday as day for change, 21
Tie, backwards, 8
Ties, drawing, 130-31

Time bombs, 102, 109-10
Toast with raspberry jam, 11-12
Toothpicks in cake, 95
Traditions, definitions and effects of, 1-4
Traveling: to cabin, 48-50; with children, 73-74; planning for, 74, 81-82; activities while, 75-77; to nearby places, 78-79; ideas for, 80-81
Tree, Christmas. *See* Christmas tree
Tree, painting of, 55
Trip book, 76
Trips. *See* Traveling
Trunk, antique, 123
T-shirts for family members, 84
Tune, naming, 69
Twelve days before Christmas, 118

Valentine lady, 102
Valentine's Day traditions, 102-3, 153
Van Dyke, Henry, 123
Vassilopitta ceremony, 99-100
Village, building, 126

Waking up of parents, 133
Wall, memory, 54-55
Washington's birthday, 104
Water, teaspoon of, 14-15
Water fights, 84
Wedding traditions, 83-86
Wednesday Surprise, 12
Weight, guessing baby's, 87
Welcoming back, 77
Wells, Evelyn, 89
Whistle, secret, 13-14
Window glass candy, 137-38
Windows, washing, 51
Winter, burning, in effigy, 110
Wish cards, 116
Work, exclusion from, 58-59
Working for free, 37
Wreath, advent, 121